Puffin Books

The Young Puffin Book of Bible Stories
Told by Pat Alexander

The Bible contains some of the greatest stories ever told. In vivid and easily understood language, Pat Alexander retells more than fifty of the most famous and best-loved. Just some of the colourful and exciting stories from the Old Testament included are those of Noah and the flood, Joshua and the battle of Jericho, David and Goliath, Daniel in the lions' den and Jonah and the whale.

At the centre of the New Testament of course is Jesus Christ. As well as the wonder of his birth and the drama of his suffering, death and resurrection, here are the stories of the parables he told – the good Samaritan, the prodigal son – and the miracles he worked.

Faithful to the original, these stories are highly entertaining and at the same time convey the Bible's timeless message of God's love for his people.

Pat Alexander and her husband founded the specialist Christian publishers, Lion Publishing. She remains its editorial director and is also the author of *The Puffin Children's Bible*.

Also retold by Pat Alexander

The Puffin Children's Bible

THE YOUNG PUFFIN BOOK OF
BIBLE STORIES

Told by Pat Alexander
Illustrated by Anthony Kerins

PUFFIN BOOKS

PUFFIN BOOKS

Published by the Penguin Group
27 Wrights Lane, London W8 5TZ, England
Viking Penguin Inc., 40 West 23rd Street, New York, New York 10010, USA
Penguin Books Australia Ltd, Ringwood, Victoria, Australia
Penguin Books Canada Ltd, 2801 John Street, Markham, Ontario, Canada L3R 1B4
Penguin Books (NZ) Ltd, 182–190 Wairau Road, Auckland 10, New Zealand

Penguin Books Ltd, Registered Offices: Harmondsworth, Middlesex, England

First published (in colour) by Lion Publishing 1983
Published in Puffin Books 1988
5 7 9 10 8 6

Text copyright © Lion Publishing, 1983
Illustrations copyright © Anthony Kerins, 1988
All rights reserved

Printed and bound in Great Britain by
Cox & Wyman Ltd, Reading
Typeset in Linotron Baskerville by
Rowland Phototypesetting Ltd
Bury St Edmunds, Suffolk

Contents

THE OLD TESTAMENT

THE NEW TESTAMENT

*This story is in all four Gospels

Stories from
THE OLD
TESTAMENT

The making and the spoiling of the world
and how God chose a people for himself
to love him and make him known

How the World was Made

Long, long ago there was no world – no sky, no sea, no land, no people.

In the beginning, God made the universe. It was completely dark. There was no sound to be heard.

Then, out of the darkness, breaking the silence, God spoke.

'Let there be light!' God said. And there was light. The light was good. God called it 'day', and he kept the dark for night. That was the first day.

Then God said, 'Let there be space around the world!' And it was so. God called the space around the world 'sky'. That was the second day.

Then God said, 'Let all the water come together away from the land!' And it was so. God called the land 'earth' and the water 'sea'.

And God saw that it was good.

But the land was brown and bare. Nothing grew. So God said, 'Let there be all kinds of plants and trees!' And the world became green with growing things – fruit and flowers and vegetables.

And God saw that it was good. That was the third day.

Then God said, 'Let there be lights in the sky to shine on the earth by day and night!' And it was so. One of the lights he called 'sun' – that was for the daytime. The other he called 'moon' – that was for the night-time. He made the twinkling stars.

And God saw that it was good. That was the fourth day.

Then God said, 'Let there be fish in the sea and birds in the air!' He made all kinds of water creatures, big and small, from the monster whale to the tiniest crab. He made all kinds of birds, big and small, from the great albatross to the tiniest humming-bird. Sparrows too! The fish splashed and the birds sang and the world was alive with sound.

And God saw that it was good. 'Let the fish fill the sea. Let the birds lay eggs and have chicks,' he said, 'and fill the world.' That was the fifth day.

Then God said, 'Let the earth produce all kinds of animals, wild and tame, big and small!' And it was so. God made them all and he saw that it was good.

'Now,' God said, 'the world is ready. Let there be people! They will be like me. And I shall put them in charge of all the creatures I have made.'

So God made people. He made them like himself. He made man and woman.

'You are to have children,' he said, 'to live in every part of the world. And I am putting you in charge of everything: the water and the land, the plants and the fish and the birds and the animals. They are all yours. Look after them for me.'

God saw all that he had made and it was very good. That was the sixth day.

So the whole universe was finished. And on the seventh day God did no work. He rested and enjoyed it all. That is why he made the seventh day a special day, for ever.

How the World was Spoiled

God made a garden in Eden. It was a beautiful garden full of trees, with a river running through. God gave the garden to the man – Adam – to look after. And God brought all the animals to Adam to see what he would call them. Adam gave names to all the animals: sheep and cow, lion and tiger, rabbit and mouse. And snake.

Adam loved God. He loved the garden. He loved the animals. But he was lonely without a friend. God knew he would be – until there was a woman too. When God made Eve, Adam was completely happy. Now there was someone to talk to, someone to share things with. Everything was perfect.

But not for long.

There was one thing – only one thing – God said that Adam must not do. There was a special tree in the middle of the garden. It was called 'the-tree-of-the-knowledge-of-good-and-evil'.

'You must not eat the fruit on that tree,' God said. 'If you do, you will die.'

One day the snake, who was the slipperiest, cunningest of all God's creatures, came to Eve and began to

ask her about the tree-of-the-knowledge-of-good-and-evil.

'Did God say you'd die if you ate the fruit? You won't die!' he said. 'It will make you wise, as wise as God himself. That's why he doesn't want you to eat it.'

Eve listened to the silky-smooth voice of the snake.

Eve looked at the fruit. It was so good her mouth began to water. And she wanted to be wise, like God.

Eve reached up and touched the fruit – and before she could think it was in her mouth.

She gave some to Adam, and he ate it too.

Then they both knew they had made a terrible mistake.

God had made them. He had given them everything. He was their friend. And they had deliberately dis-obeyed him.

That evening, when God came to the garden to see them, they hid.

But no one can hide from God.

He knew at once that they had disobeyed.

'Did you eat the fruit I told you not to eat?' God asked the man.

'The woman gave it to me,' Adam said, making excuses. 'And I ate.'

'Why did you do it?' God asked the woman.

Eve hung her head, ashamed. 'It was the snake,' she whispered, making excuses.

God punished the snake.

But Adam and Eve had to leave the garden for ever.

Everything was spoiled because the man and the woman disobeyed God.

The Flood – and a Rainbow

Adam and Eve left the garden of Eden. Children were born and grew up. Old people died – as God had said. Many years went by, and there were many people in God's world. But they fought and stole. They were cruel and unkind. They told lies. Not one of them thought about God or listened to him. When God saw what was happening, how the people were spoiling his world, he was sad. He knew he would have to start all over again.

But there was one man, Noah, who loved God and listened to him, and did as God said.

So God said to him, 'Noah, you must build a strong boat – a big one with room for all your family, and for two of every kind of animal. Very soon I shall send rain and there will be a great flood. Every creature on earth will drown – except you and your family and the birds and animals. You will be safe, if you do as I say.'

Noah did as God said. Everyone laughed when they saw him. 'A boat? Here? Miles from the sea?' But Noah took no notice. He just did as God said.

At last the boat was ready.

'In seven days the rain will come,' God said. 'Take

two of every kind of bird and animal and settle them inside. And take plenty of food.'

Noah did as God told him.

Last of all he and his family went on board.

People were still laughing when the first black rain-cloud moved across the sky. Big drops of rain bounced down on to the hard dry earth. Everyone ran indoors.

Lightning flashed. Thunder crashed. Little puddles became big puddles. Big puddles became lakes. And the lakes became a wide rising sea.

The flood lifted Noah's boat and carried it high above the houses and fields. High above the woods and hills. High above the highest mountain. Soon there was no dry ground left. The flood covered everything. No one, nothing, was left alive – except on Noah's boat. God kept Noah, and his family, and all the birds and animals safe.

For forty days it rained. Then the rain stopped and God sent a dry wind. Slowly, slowly the water began to go down.

Bump! The boat touched land. It was resting on the side of a mountain. But there was still a sea of water all around. On board, everyone began to get irritable. They were so tired of being shut up. How much longer?

Noah sent out a dove. She flew around and came back. The trees were still under water. Seven days later Noah sent her out again. This time she came back with a fresh green leaf in her beak. Everyone cheered: 'Hurray! Not long now.'

At last God spoke to Noah. 'It's time to leave,' he said. They took off the cover and opened the door. The muddy water had gone. The sun shone. The world looked green and new. There was a great rush to get out. The animals jumped for joy and the birds all sang at once. As for Noah and his family, 'Thank you, oh thank you, God,' they said. It was so good to feel the firm ground under their feet and smell the flowers.

'Look up at the sky,' God said to Noah. And there overhead was a glorious rainbow.

'I will never again send a flood to destroy the world,' God said. 'The rainbow in the sky will remind me of my promise.'

The Promise

God kept his promise to Noah.

Noah's three sons and their wives had children, and their children had children . . . Many years went by.

In the land we call Iraq, in the town of Ur, there lived a man called Abraham. He had a wife whose name was Sarah. But Abraham and Sarah had no children. They were very sad about that.

One day God spoke to Abraham.

'I want you to go on a journey,' he said, 'to a new country. Just you and Sarah, not the rest of the family. That new country is going to belong to your descendants. You are going to be famous. I'm going to make you the father of a great nation.'

Abraham and Sarah were quite old. But they did as God said. They said goodbye to all the family except one nephew called Lot, and they set off with their servants and their sheep and goats, and tents to sleep in. They were going to the land that we call Israel. It was a long, long way. And they didn't know anyone there. They were just doing as God said. God would look after them.

When they got to the land of Israel they still had to live in tents, moving from place to place to find fresh grass and water for the animals.

God had promised to make Abraham the father of a great nation. But twenty-four years went by and still they had no children, though God kept saying, 'Look at the sky and try to count the stars. You will have as many descendants as that! Think how many grains of sand there are. I will give you as many descendants as that! And this whole land will be yours.'

But still Abraham and Sarah had no children. And they did not own the land – not even a field to build a house on. And by now they were very old.

Then one hot afternoon three visitors came. Abraham did not know them. But he ran to make them welcome. And Sarah quickly got them a meal.

After they had eaten, one of the men said: 'Nine

months from now I will come back, and your wife Sarah
will have a son.'

Abraham was sure that this was a message from God.
Sarah wanted – so much – to believe what he said. But it
was quite impossible now. She was too old to have a
baby.

She *was* too old – but she was wrong about the baby.

Nothing is impossible for God.

God always keeps his promises.

Nine months from that day Sarah's baby son was
born. She cuddled him in her arms, this miracle baby,
and cried for joy. And Abraham was ready to burst with
pride. A son, at last!

They decided to call him Isaac.

No baby ever had a mother and father who loved him
more.

A Hard Test

Like every other baby, Isaac soon began to grow.

He cut his first tooth.

He took his first wobbly step.

He learned his first words.

Sarah and Abraham watched him grow up. They laughed with him. They played with him. When he was sick they worried about him. They loved their little son so much. He was the only one. Sarah had no other children. Every day they thanked God for him.

God had promised them a son, and he had kept his promise. God had promised to make Abraham the

father of a great nation and to give him the land of Israel. He would keep those promises too.

Then one day a terrible thing happened.

God said to Abraham, 'You are to take your son Isaac, your only son, whom you love so much, to the land of Moriah, and offer him as a sacrifice to me.'

Kill his son? A sharp pain stabbed through Abraham's heart. How could he do it? But he had always done as God said. And God had always been right.

Although Abraham did not know it, God was setting him a test, the hardest he would ever have. God asks us to love him first, more even than those we love best. He wanted to be sure that little Isaac had not taken first place – the place that belongs to God – in his father's heart.

God did not want a human sacrifice. But Abraham did not know that. In his day most people thought they could please their gods by offering their children in sacrifice.

Abraham faced God's test. And he did not fail. Early next morning he set out with Isaac for the land of Moriah. He took with him his knife, and wood for the fire, and burning coals to light it.

Isaac was puzzled.

'Father,' he asked, 'where is the lamb for the sacrifice?'

Abraham's throat tightened. He could hardly speak. Somehow he managed to find his voice.

'God will provide it.'

When they came to the place, Abraham piled up

stones to make an altar, and arranged the wood on the stones. He tied Isaac's hands and feet, and placed him on top. He drew his knife . . .

Then God spoke: 'Don't hurt the boy. Set him free. Now I know how much you love me.'

Abraham looked round, and there in a bush was a ram, caught by its horns. He had been right. God himself had provided the sacrifice.

Abraham killed the ram, and roasted it on the altar.

'Because of this,' God said, 'because you were pre-pared even to lose your son if that was what I asked, I promise again: I will give you as many descendants as there are stars in the sky, or grains of sand on the seashore – because you did as I said and trusted me.'

Then Abraham took Isaac safely home again.

A Very Brave Girl

Abraham had been worried for some time. He was very old. Sarah, his wife, had died. And Isaac – grown up now – was still not married. The right wife was very important. For God had promised that Abraham would become the father of a great nation, living in the land of Israel.

In those days, as in many countries today, it was the fathers and mothers who arranged the weddings. So Abraham called his chief servant to him.

'I am too old for long journeys,' he said, 'so I want you to go to the country where I was born, to my family, and choose a wife for Isaac. He must stay here. Promise me you will do it.'

The servant's heart sank. To go all that way. What if the girl would not leave her family to marry a man she had never seen? But he promised to do as Abraham said.

He set off on the long journey, taking a few men with him and ten camels to carry the food and the presents.

It was late afternoon, many days later, when he arrived. The camels were thirsty, so he stopped at the

well outside the town, where the girls came to fill up
their water-jars. He had thought a lot about it. He knew
just what to do. But it would only work if God helped
him.

'Lord God of my master Abraham,' he said. 'I'm
asking you to keep your promise to my master. I shall
say to one of these girls, "Please put down your water-
jar and give me a drink." Let the one who offers to water
the camels too be the one you have chosen as Isaac's
wife.'

While he was still speaking, Rebecca arrived with her
water-jar on her shoulder. She was very beautiful.
When the servant asked her for a drink, she smiled and
said, 'Let me water your camels too. They must be
thirsty.' Abraham's servant took two gold bracelets
from his bag and put them on her arms.

'Please tell me who your father is,' he said.

When he heard that Rebecca's father was Abraham's own nephew he was amazed. God had led him straight to the girl he had chosen to be Isaac's wife.

Rebecca ran to tell her family, and her brother Laban came out to welcome the visitor. When they were sitting down to a meal, he explained why he had come. He told them about the promise he had made to Abraham, and his prayer to God at the well.

The family listened in silence.

'This is God's doing,' they said. 'How can we say no? Rebecca can go with you to marry Isaac.'

Then Abraham's servant brought out the presents: lovely clothes and bracelets of gold and silver for Rebecca, and expensive gifts for her mother too.

Next day he was eager to set off home. The family thought it was too soon. But they let Rebecca decide.

'Do you want to go with this man?'

'Yes,' she answered. Rebecca was a very brave girl.

So they set out on the long journey.

Isaac was out walking in the fields early one evening when he saw the camels coming.

At last Isaac and Rebecca met.

Isaac loved his new wife. And Rebecca, though she missed her family, did not regret the brave moment when she said, 'Yes.'

Cheat!

Isaac and Rebecca had twin sons. Esau, the one born first, was tough. He loved to be out of doors and became a good hunter. Isaac was proud of him. He enjoyed the tasty stews Rebecca made from the meat Esau brought home. The younger twin, Jacob, was quiet and thoughtful. He preferred to stay at home. His mother loved him best.

Esau was noisy and careless.

Jacob was clever and cunning – always trying to be one up on his brother.

It wasn't a very happy home.

Isaac was a rich man. Esau, because he was born first, would have most when his father died. In those days, just before the father of the family died, he would ask God's special blessing on the eldest son. It was a kind of guarantee of good things to come. And it was only for the eldest.

Isaac grew old and went blind.

One day he called Esau to him. 'I want you to go out hunting. Bring back some venison for a tasty stew – and I will give you my special blessing.'

But Rebecca overheard. She wanted that special blessing for Jacob. Esau didn't care about it. Why should he have it? They were twins, after all.

'There's no time to lose,' she said to Jacob. 'Bring me two young goats. I will make a stew, just as your father likes it. You can take it in, and he will give *you* the blessing.'

'But he'll know I'm not Esau,' Jacob protested. 'My skin is smooth, not rough and hairy like his.' (Jacob didn't mind cheating. He just didn't want to be found out.)

'Do as I say,' Rebecca told him.

So she cooked the stew, just as Isaac liked it. Then she tied the hairy skins of the goats on Jacob's arms and neck to make him feel like Esau. And Jacob went in to his father.

'Are you Jacob or Esau?' Isaac asked.

'I am your elder son, Esau,' Jacob lied. 'Sit up and enjoy the stew I've brought. Then you can give me your blessing.'

'You've been very quick,' Isaac said.

'God helped me,' lied Jacob.

'Let me touch you. Are you really Esau? The voice is Jacob's but the arms feel like Esau's.'

'I am Esau, Father.'

So Jacob tricked his blind old father, and cheated his brother Esau. And Isaac gave Jacob the blessing.

'May God give you good crops. May he give you plenty of corn and wine. May nations be your servants. May you rule over all your family.'

Jacob went out.

A little while later, Esau came to his father.

'Sit up and enjoy the stew I've brought. Then you can give me your blessing.' But he was too late.

Jacob had tricked his blind old father, and cheated his brother Esau. But it did him no good. Esau hated Jacob from that day – and vowed to kill him.

Jacob had to run for his life.

He had to leave the home he loved. He had to leave his mother and go right away, where Esau would not follow him.

How God
Took Care of Jacob

Jacob was running away. He was going to stay with his Uncle Laban. He was afraid of Esau; afraid of the journey; afraid of what Uncle Laban would say. Jacob was alone and afraid. And God knew.

When night fell, Jacob had to stop running. He lay down on the ground to sleep. And he had a very strange dream.

He was at the bottom of some stairs. The top was in heaven. And there were angels going up and down them.

Then God came and stood beside him. 'I am the Lord, the God of Abraham and Isaac. I will give this land to you and your descendants. I will be with you wherever you go, and I will bring you safely home.'

When he woke up, Jacob knew it wasn't just a dream. God really had been talking to him. God knew he had lied and cheated but he would still take care of him.

So Jacob made God a promise in return. 'If you do all that you have said, and bring me safely home, you won't be just the God of Abraham and Isaac – you will be *my* God.'

He felt much better after that!

Before long he was telling his Uncle Laban the whole story. Uncle Laban – and beautiful cousin Rachel. But Uncle Laban, like Jacob, was clever and cunning – and a cheat.

Jacob fell in love with his cousin Rachel. He said to his uncle, 'I will look after your flocks for nothing for seven years, if you will let me marry Rachel.'

Laban agreed. But when the wedding came, he cheated. The girl behind the long veil was not beautiful Rachel. It was her older sister, Leah, whom no one wanted to marry.

So Jacob looked after the flocks for nothing for another seven years, and married Rachel too.

Now he had two wives, but neither of them was

happy. Leah was unhappy because her husband did not love her. Rachel was unhappy because Leah had children, but she had none.

The years went by and Jacob had six sons and a daughter from Leah, and – at last – one little son, called Joseph, from Rachel. But still he looked after Laban's flocks and had nothing of his own.

'What shall I pay you?' Laban asked at last.

'Let me have a share of the flock,' Jacob said. 'All the black lambs and all the spotted goats.'

Laban tried to cheat again. But this time he did not win. God was looking after Jacob. And when the new lambs were born, there were lots of black ones. Lots of spotted goats too.

Now that he had flocks of his own it was time for Jacob to go. So they packed their things and set out.

Jacob had worked for Laban for twenty years. For twenty years Laban had tried to trick and cheat him. But God had always looked after Jacob. Now he had something special to tell him.

'I am going to change your name,' God said. 'From now on you won't be Jacob, the cheat. Your name will be Israel.' (That is how Jacob's people came to be called 'the people of Israel'.) 'And you don't need to worry about Esau,' God said. (He knew how scared Jacob was.)

The very next day, Jacob and Esau met – and their old quarrel was forgotten. Esau hugged Jacob, and Jacob hugged Esau. He was forgiven.

The Jealous Brothers

Jacob had twelve fine sons. There were Leah's ten boys. And there was Rachel's boy, Joseph. Jacob's heart warmed at the thought of Joseph. He loved him more than all the others put together – and they knew it. The twelfth son, Benjamin, was special too – but he was still very young. (Rachel had died when Benjamin was born.)

Jacob had a special coat made for Joseph – a very fine coat with long sleeves. Not the kind of thing to wear for minding the sheep! And that was what the rest of them had to do – out in the baking sun all day, tramping long miles, fighting off wolves and bears. How they hated daddy's little pet – his precious Joseph. It was bad enough to have him telling tales. But then he began to tell them his dreams.

'Listen, everyone. I had this dream. We were out in the fields tying up the sheaves. And your sheaves all bowed down to mine. What do you think of that?'

The brothers could hardly bear to speak to him.

'Listen, everyone. I had this dream. I saw the sun, the moon and eleven stars bow down to me.'

This was too much, even for his father.

'What kind of dream is that? Do you think your brothers and Leah and I are going to come and bow down to you?' The anger in his voice took Joseph by surprise.

One day, when the brothers were miles away with the flock, Joseph was sent to find them.

They saw him coming a long way off. With that coat on, it wasn't hard to spot him! Suddenly all their jealousy burst out. They hated Joseph. They wished he were dead. But how could they get rid of him?

'Let's kill him and throw his body down that dried-up well,' one of them said. 'We can say a wild animal killed him.'

'No, don't let's hurt him,' Reuben said. 'Let's just leave him there for a bit to teach him a lesson.' (Reuben was hoping to be able to rescue Joseph and send him back home.)

When Joseph reached them they tore off that special coat of his and threw him into the well.

They were eating a meal – all except Reuben – when the traders came past on their way to Egypt. Their swaying camels were loaded with spices and sweet-smelling perfumes.

Judah had a brainwave. 'Let's sell Joseph to those traders,' he said. 'Then we won't have to hurt him. He is our brother, after all.'

And that is what they did. They pulled Joseph out of the well and sold him to the traders for twenty silver coins. The traders took Joseph to Egypt. Reuben came back too late to save him.

And that was the last the brothers saw of Joseph – for a very long time. But it wasn't the last of him. God saw to that.

The cruel brothers took home Joseph's coat, all stained with blood. They wanted their father to think that some wild animal had killed him.

The King's Dream

In Egypt Joseph was sold to a captain of the palace guard. He worked hard and did well. Soon he was put in charge of everything. But the captain's spiteful wife told lies about him. She had Joseph arrested and put in prison.

All the time – even when he was a slave, even when he was in prison – God was looking after Joseph.

Joseph didn't have dreams in prison. But the other prisoners did. They felt sure that their dreams meant something. And they were right. God showed Joseph what those dreams meant – and what he said came true.

One day the king himself had a dream. That was how Joseph got out of prison. The king felt sure his dream meant something. But no one could tell him what – until they remembered Joseph.

'Send for him at once,' said the king. But, of course, no one goes straight from prison to see a king. So Joseph had a good wash first, and put on clean clothes. Then he went to see the king.

'I've been told you can tell the meaning of dreams,' the king said. 'Can you tell me what mine means?'

'*I* can't,' Joseph said. 'But God can.'

So the king told him his dream.

'I was standing on the bank of the River Nile,' he said, 'and seven fat cows came out of the river to graze. Then seven of the thinnest, boniest cows I have ever seen came and ate up the seven fat cows. But afterwards they were just as thin as before.

'After that, I saw seven fat heads of grain – and seven thin heads that ate them up. Can you explain?'

'Both dreams mean the same thing,' Joseph said. 'For seven years there will be good harvests with plenty of everything. After that will come seven years of hunger. Crops will fail. There will be nothing to eat. Everyone will be hungry and Egypt will be ruined. It's going to happen soon.

'I think you should put the best man you have in charge. He can make sure you store enough food in the good years to feed everyone when the hungry years come.'

'We shall never find a better man than you,' said the king. 'You have told me the meaning of my dream. I can see that God is with you. You shall be the new governor of Egypt.'

So the king put his ring with the royal seal on Joseph's finger. He gave him fine new clothes and placed a gold chain around his neck. He even gave him his second-best chariot to ride in!

Joseph was only seventeen when his brothers sold him. He was thirty when the king made him governor of Egypt.

The Missing Silver Cup

They had never known such harvests! For seven years Joseph stored up grain – in the cities of Egypt – great golden heaps of it. Then the hungry years began. There was plenty of food in Egypt, but in Israel Joseph's brothers did not have enough to eat.

'I hear there is grain in Egypt,' their father Jacob said. 'Go and buy some, or we shall starve.' None of them knew that Joseph was governor of Egypt. They all thought he was dead.

When they arrived Joseph's brothers bowed low before him. He knew them at once, but pretended not to. There were things he wanted to find out.

'Foreign spies!' he said fiercely.

'No sir, we're honest men. There were twelve of us brothers. But one is dead now and the youngest is at home with our father.'

'Spies!' Joseph insisted. And he put them in prison. Three days later he made them an offer. 'I will give you a chance to prove your story. If one of you stays here, in prison, the rest can go home. But don't come back without your youngest brother.' He chose Simeon to stay.

Joseph ordered his men to fill his brothers' sacks with grain, and to put their money back inside. On the way home they found the money. Now they really were in trouble!

Jacob listened to their story. But he would not let Benjamin go. 'Do you want me to lose all my children? First Joseph, then Simeon, now Benjamin. If anything happens to him, it will kill me.'

But soon they had used up all the grain. They had to go back taking Benjamin with them.

'I promise I'll keep him safe,' Judah said.

So they set off, with presents for the governor, and money to pay for both lots of grain.

When Joseph saw Benjamin with them he ordered his servants to prepare a meal and brought the brothers into his house. They were very frightened. They tried to explain about the money. But the servant in charge said that he'd been paid.

'Your God must have returned the money to you,' he said. And he brought Simeon to them.

Then they gave Joseph their presents and knelt before him. When he saw Benjamin, Joseph almost cried.

They were on their way home when Joseph's men caught up with them. 'You have stolen the governor's silver cup! Open your sacks!'

They opened their sacks. Joseph had ordered his men to hide the cup in Benjamin's sack – and there it was. The brothers were horrified.

'The one who stole my cup shall be my slave,' Joseph

said. 'The rest of you may go free.' (He was testing them.)

But the brothers refused to go. 'This will kill our father,' Judah said. 'Let me stay instead. Please let Benjamin go.'

Then Joseph knew that his brothers were really sorry for what they had done to him. 'I am your brother Joseph,' he said – and he burst into tears. 'Don't blame yourselves. God sent me here to save all our lives. Hurry home and tell my father. Then you must all come here to live. There are five more hungry years to come.'

Then he threw his arms around Benjamin and hugged him. The brothers all laughed and cried together and everyone talked at once.

So the people of Israel came to live in Egypt.

The Secret Baby

Hundreds of years went by. There was a new king in Egypt who didn't remember Joseph. The new king made the people of Israel his slaves.

In a little house by the River Nile a baby was born. But he had to be kept secret. No one must know. He must not cry. He must not laugh. If some one heard him, they would tell the king. And the great king of Egypt had given his people a terrible command.

'Take every baby boy born to the people of Israel and throw him into the River Nile to drown.'

The new baby's mother and father, and big sister Miriam, loved him very much. They were all so afraid for their baby. They kept him secret for three long months. Every time he began to cry, Miriam ran to cuddle him close. But they knew they could not keep him quiet much longer.

So they thought of a plan.

Miriam picked some of the tall reeds that grew by the river. And her mother made them into a little basket-cradle just big enough for the baby. She put thick tar on the bottom to make it watertight. And she made a lid that let in air.

Then she kissed the baby and put him in the basket. They carried it down to the river and put it among the reeds at the river's edge. Miriam hid close by, to watch.

Only one person could defy the king's command and save the baby's life. That was the king's own daughter.

Every day the princess of Egypt came down to the river to bathe. She noticed the basket at once. One of her servants brought it to her. She opened the lid – and at that very moment the baby began to cry.

Miriam held her breath.

'Poor little thing,' the princess said. 'He must be hungry.'

Miriam ran up. 'Shall I fetch someone to feed him?'

'Yes, please,' said the princess. She'd never looked after a baby before. But she loved this baby as soon as she saw him.

So Miriam went to fetch – the baby's own mother!

'Look after him for me,' the princess said. 'I will pay you well.'

The plan had worked!

The baby was looked after by his own mother in his own home till he was big enough to go the palace. Then the princess made him her adopted son. She called him Moses.

Rescue!

One day when Moses was grown up he saw one of the cruel Egyptian slave-drivers kill an Israelite. Moses hit the Egyptian so hard that he killed him. Then he ran away to the desert where no one would find him.

One day, out there in the desert, Moses saw a very strange thing. A bush was on fire. He could see the flames, but there was no smoke – and the leaves weren't burning.

Then he heard a voice, calling him. 'Moses, listen to me. I am God – the God of Abraham, Isaac and Jacob. I

have seen the Egyptians' cruel whips. I have heard my people cry out for help. I am sending you to rescue them.'

'Sending *me*? How can I possibly go to the king of Egypt?' Moses said.

'I shall be with you,' God said. 'I will tell you what to do. And you can take your brother Aaron. He's good at speaking.'

So Moses and Aaron went to the king of Egypt. They spoke to him politely. 'Your Majesty,' they said, 'we have a message for you from God – the God of Israel. He says will you please give his people time off to go and worship him in the desert?'

'The God of Israel? Who is he? I don't know him,' the king said rudely. And he ordered his men to make the people of Israel work harder than ever.

Moses and Aaron were very upset. They had only made things worse. But not even a king can upset God's plans.

'I have given the king of Egypt his chance,' God said. 'Now I shall *make* him let my people go. They will leave his land for ever. But first you must go back and warn him.'

Next morning Moses and Aaron met the king again, down by the river. 'God, the God of Israel, says: "Let my people go. Or I will turn this river into blood."'

The king took no notice. So God turned the river into blood. But still the king said no.

A week later, God sent Moses and Aaron to the king again. 'God, the God of Israel, says: "Let my people go. Or I will send a plague of frogs."'

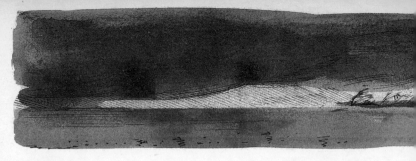

The king took no notice. So God sent a plague of frogs. There were frogs in the beds, frogs in the flour, frogs in the cooking-pots.

'Take the frogs away,' said the king. But when all the frogs had gone he still said no.

So God sent gnats – great clouds of them. The gnats bit. The people scratched. But still the king said no.

Then God sent flies.

And after that, the cattle died.

Everyone had boils.

Hail beat the grain flat.

Locusts ate up every blade of grass.

For three terrible days the land was as dark as night. No one could see. But still the king said no.

'Get out of my sight,' he said to Moses and Aaron. 'I never want to see you again.'

So God gave his last warning and sent his last punishment. That night the eldest son in every house in

Egypt died. Only God's people were safe: death 'passed over' them. In the palace the king's eldest son died. It was the worst thing that had ever happened in Egypt. And it was the king's own fault.

Then, at last, the king relented. He sent for Moses and Aaron. 'Get out of Egypt,' he shouted, 'you and your people. Go and worship your God.' And then he added quietly, 'And ask your God to bless me.'

So God's people left Egypt – men and women and children; sheep and goats and cattle. They set out on the long walk across the desert to the Red Sea.

The Great Escape

It was strangely quiet in the land of Egypt. No bricks were made; no building was done. The people of Israel – all the slaves – had gone!

Then the king of Egypt had second thoughts. It wasn't too late. There was still time to get them back. The Israelites were walking. They couldn't have got far.

'Call in the army! Fetch the horses! Get out the chariots! After them!'

There was a great cloud of dust in the desert. It was moving fast. No one knew who saw it first, but soon everyone was looking back, trying to make it out. Then a gust of wind blew the dust clear. The people of Israel could see. Horses and chariots. Hundreds of them! It was the king of Egypt's army.

With the army behind them, and the sea in front, the Israelites were trapped. Everyone began to panic. They turned on Moses, shouting at him.

'Look what you've done. Why didn't you leave us in Egypt? Now we'll all be killed. What are we going to do?'

'Nothing at all,' Moses answered calmly – when he could make himself heard. 'God rescued us from Egypt. He won't let us die here. We must just wait and see what he does.'

It wasn't easy. They felt so frightened. How long would it take those chariots to catch up with them?

But they needn't have worried. God made sure the army did not reach them. He put a thick dark cloud between the Egyptians and the people of Israel.

Then God said to Moses: 'Stretch your arm out over the sea.' Moses did as he was told. And God sent a strong east wind. All night long it blew against the sea, piling up the water. Before long there was a clear path all the way across. All the Israelites had to do was walk to the other side.

But at dawn, when the king of Egypt's army tried to follow, their chariot wheels got stuck.

God said to Moses again: 'Stretch your arm out over the sea.' Moses did as he was told. The wind dropped and the water flooded back. One minute the Egyptian army was there. The next it was gone – lost in the swirling water.

The Israelites, watching anxiously from the far side, gave a great cheer. They were safe! It was such a relief they burst out singing.

'Who can work miracles like the God of Israel? He will be our king for ever.'

Tents in the Desert

The people of Israel were hungry and thirsty. God had rescued them from Egypt. They were free. He was taking them to a new land. But they had to cross the desert first.

'We shall starve in this desert,' they said. 'We were never hungry in Egypt.' They forgot how unhappy they had been. They forgot the cruel lash of the whip. They were really very ungrateful.

But God was not going to let them starve. He knew there was no grain to make bread in the desert. So he gave them special food called 'manna'.

Each morning, as the hot sun dried up the dew, there was the manna like frost on the ground. They only had to pick it up and share it out. It tasted a bit like honey.

Next they grumbled because there was no meat. And God sent a flock of birds called quails. The birds were so tired from their long flight that they were easy to catch. There was plenty for everyone.

When the people were thirsty God found water for them. All the time they were in the desert he looked after them. And they were there a very long time.

In Egypt the people had lived in houses. But in the desert everyone lived in tents. They moved from place to place to find food and water for their flocks.

God had a tent too, though he didn't live in it in the way we do. He was there – but he was everywhere else too. God's tent stood right in the middle of the camp, so that the people would know God was with them. It was a very beautiful tent. There were thick goatskin covers on the outside. But the hangings inside were made of fine linen – blue and purple and red – embroidered all over. The tent had two rooms.

God gave certain rules to his people in the desert, important rules which they had to keep. (We call them the Ten Commandments.) A copy of those laws was kept in a special box – 'the ark of the covenant' – in the private inside room in God's tent.

It was the priests' job to look after God's tent. No one else could touch it or go inside. Not even the priests were allowed inside the little private room, it was so special. God said the High Priest could go in, but only once a year.

In the desert, at Mount Sinai, God made his people a promise.

'If you obey me, if you keep the laws of my kingdom, you will be my own people. The whole world is mine, but you will be my chosen people.'

'We promise to do as you say,' they answered. 'You have rescued us from Egypt. We want to be your people.'

But they soon broke their promise.

So God said they must stay in the desert for forty years. They weren't ready yet for the new land he had promised them.

Catch Those Spies!

The people of Israel had a new leader. His name was Joshua.

'Be brave!' God said to him. 'Be strong. I shall be with you as I was with Moses. Just make sure you do as I say. It's time to leave the desert. You must lead my people into the land I promised them.'

But people were saying that the promised land, the land of Canaan that we now call Israel, was a land full of giants. And it's hard to be brave when there are giants to fight. So Joshua chose two men to go across the river and find out.

'Spy out the land,' Joshua said to them. 'Find out all you can about Jericho – that strong walled city over there. And make sure no one catches you!'

So the two men set off, in disguise, so that no one would know they were Israelites.

When they got to Jericho, they stayed at the house of a woman called Rahab. But somehow the king of Jericho got to hear about them. Before long the king's men were hammering at Rahab's door. 'Open up! Open up! Those two men staying with you – they're spies. Bring them out!'

But Rahab didn't hand the spies over. Instead she hid them under some piles of flax put out to dry on the flat roof of her house.

'Some men did come here,' she said to the king's men. 'I don't know where they were from. But they left before the city gates closed at sunset. If you hurry you may still catch them.'

The king's men left the city.

And Rahab climbed the stairs to the flat roof. 'You can come out now,' she said to the spies. 'It's quite safe. I know that God has given you this land. We have all heard how he dried up the Red Sea for you to cross. Everyone is afraid of you – because your God is the God of heaven and earth. That's why I saved your lives. Now promise me that I and my family will be safe when you take the city.'

Rahab's house was built into the thick outside wall of the city. So when it was dark she let down a rope from the window and the two men slid to the ground.

'Hide for a few days,' she said, 'then, when the hunt has died down, you'll be able to go back safely to your people.'

'Thank you for all you've done,' the two men said. 'When the time comes, get your family together, here in the house. And tie this red cord in the window where our soldiers can see it. Then we promise you'll be safe.' And they crept away into the darkness.

A few days later they were back in the camp, reporting to Joshua. 'No need to be afraid of giants,' they said. 'Everyone over there is shaking in his shoes. God has given us the land – all we have to do is march in and take it.'

The Day
the Walls Fell Down

The people of Israel were camping close to the River
Jordan. They were ready to go across as soon as God
gave the word.

The river was deep and wide. Only a few of them
could swim, and there were lots of toddlers and babies –
not to mention all the animals and baggage. There was
no bridge and there were no boats either. It was like the
time they crossed the Red Sea, only this time the enemy
was in front instead of behind.

God explained his plan to Joshua. And Joshua told
the people.

'God says we are to move into the promised land,' he
said. 'And he will drive out all our enemies as we go. He
is going with us. The priests who carry the ark of God's
covenant will walk right into the river. As soon as they
step into the water the river will stop running, and you
will be able to walk across.'

So the priests who carried the ark of God's covenant
went down to the river and stepped into the water. And
at that very moment, upstream at Adam, the muddy
banks caved in with a roar, making a great dam. The

river stopped running. And the people of Israel went across, into the promised land.

They were just a few miles from the strong walled city of Jericho. Its great wooden gates were shut and barred. There were guards on the walls. No one could go in or out because the king of Jericho was afraid of the people of Israel and their amazing God.

God explained his plan to Joshua. And Joshua told the people. The orders God gave were very strange indeed! But the Israelites did exactly as he said.

Every day, for six days, the people of Israel marched right around the city of Jericho – while everyone inside watched anxiously.

A troop of soldiers led the way. Then came seven priests, each with a trumpet – blowing with all their might. Behind them came the priests who carried the ark of God's covenant. And after them marched the rest

of the army. No one shouted. No one spoke. Only the loud blast of the trumpets shattered the silence.

Every day, for six days, the same thing happened. They marched around the city once. Then they all went back to camp. The people of Jericho did not know what to make of it. But they grew more and more afraid. It was weird.

On the seventh day the Israelites were up at dawn. Once, twice, three times, four times, five times, six times – *seven* times they marched around Jericho. Then Joshua said to his men, 'God has given you the city!'

They gave a great shout.

The priests blew their trumpets.

And the huge walls of the city, walls as thick as a house, collapsed into a heap of dust and rubble.

Joshua's men went in and took the city. Only Rahab and her family were saved, because she had saved the lives of the two spies.

The Army
that Ran Away

There was no stopping Joshua and the army of Israel. North and south they marched, until the whole country was theirs. Joshua divided up the land among the twelve tribes – the descendants of Jacob's twelve sons.

'God has given us a land of our own. He has kept his promise,' Joshua said. 'We must not forget him now, or settle down with the nations around and worship their gods. If we do, there will be trouble.'

'We promise always to do as God says,' the people answered.

But after Joshua died they broke their promise. They forgot God and all he had done for them. They settled down with the nations around and worshipped their gods. And there *was* trouble.

The Ammonites and the Moabites and the Midianites all began to attack the people of Israel. And the Israelites lost. They cried out to God for help. And God heard.

He sent Gideon to the rescue. Gideon was just an ordinary farmer. He wasn't a great hero. And he took a lot of persuading. But in the end he did as God said.

Gideon called together all the fighting men of Israel and marched against the Midianites. The Israelites camped by the spring of Harod. Across the valley the Midianite tents were as thick on the ground as a plague of locusts. They rode in from the desert on camels – so many no one could count them. They made Gideon's army look very small.

But God said to Gideon, 'Your army is too big. I am going to win this battle for you. But with all these men you will think you've done it by yourselves. So you must send home everyone who is afraid.'

Gideon did as God said. Most of his soldiers were afraid. Twenty-two thousand went home.

But God said to Gideon again, 'Your army is too big. Take the men down to the water to drink. Everyone who kneels down to drink can go home. Only the ones who scoop up the water in their hands can stay.'

Gideon did as God said. That left just three hundred men to fight the Midianites.

That night God told Gideon to attack.

Gideon divided his men into three groups. He gave each man a trumpet and a jar with a burning torch inside it. Silently they crept through the darkness to the edge of the enemy's camp. They spread in a circle all around it.

Then Gideon gave the signal.

Each man blew his trumpet. Each man smashed his jar. The torches flamed in the darkness.

'A sword for God and for Gideon!' they shouted.

The Midianites were fast asleep in their tents. They leapt to their feet in fright and grabbed their swords. And in the darkness the Midianite soldiers began to fight one another! Before long the whole army ran away yelling.

Gideon and his men just stood and watched.

They knew that God had won this battle for them. His people were free again.

Samson the Superman

The Philistines were worried. They thought they had the Israelites beaten. Until they came up against Samson – Samson the superman; Samson, who could tear a lion in pieces with his bare hands; Samson, who killed a thousand Philistines single-handed.

What was the secret of his strength?

The Philistines had no idea that *God* was Samson's secret. God chose him before he was born to be the new champion of Israel; to rescue them from the Philistines. Samson was God's man. As a sign of it, his long hair was never cut.

Then Samson fell in love with beautiful Delilah. And the Philistines got their chance – because Delilah was a Philistine.

Samson's father tried to reason with him. But it was no use – he was in love!

Anything Samson did was news. So the Philistine kings soon got to hear of it. 'Five thousand pieces of silver if you can find out the secret of his strength,' they said to Delilah.

So the next time Samson came Delilah asked him,

'How could someone take you prisoner?'

'Tie me with seven new bowstrings,' Samson said, 'and I will be no stronger than anyone else.'

So Delilah tied him up with seven new bowstrings. Then she shouted, 'Samson, the Philistines are here!'

But he snapped the bowstrings like cotton.

She tried again. 'Don't tease me. How could someone take you prisoner?'

'Tie me with seven new ropes,' Samson said, 'and I will be no stronger than anyone else.'

So Delilah tied him up with seven new ropes. Then she shouted, 'Samson, the Philistines are here!'

But he snapped the ropes like cotton.

'Why won't you tell me the truth?' she begged. 'How could someone take you prisoner?'

'Weave my hair into your loom,' Samson said, 'and I will be no stronger than anyone else.'

As soon as he fell asleep Delilah wove his hair into her loom. Then she shouted, 'Samson, the Philistines are here!'

But he just shook himself free.

'How can you say you love me and not tell me the truth?' Delilah stormed. Day after day she pestered him for an answer, until at last he told her.

'I am God's man,' he said. 'My long hair is the sign of it; cut it and I will be no stronger than anyone else.'

As soon as he fell asleep Delilah called in a man to cut off Samson's hair.

'Samson, the Philistines are here!' she shouted. And this time the Philistines took him prisoner. God had taken away Samson's special strength. The Philistine soldiers blinded Samson and took him prisoner.

In prison, unable to see, Samson came to his senses. He asked God for one more chance.

The Philistines held a great feast to their god. They brought Samson out of prison. He stood between the two great pillars which held the building up, and they all jeered at him.

Samson prayed to God for strength. Then, putting one hand on each of the pillars, he pushed with all his might. The pillars trembled and shook. They began to move – and the whole building crashed to the ground, killing Samson and everyone in it.

The Voice in the Dark

Hannah had made God a promise. Her husband loved her very much, but she had no children, and she did so want a baby.

'If you answer my prayer and give me a son,' Hannah promised God, 'I will give him back, to serve you all his life.'

God did answer Hannah's prayer. He gave her a son. She called him Samuel. When Samuel was three years old Hannah kept her promise to God. She brought Samuel to God's tent at Shiloh, for Eli the priest to look after.

Eli was old and sad. He had loved and served God all his life. But his own two sons were selfish and greedy. They had no respect for God, or their father.

Little Samuel took Eli's mind off his troubles. He loved the old man, and did all he could to help him. He loved the exciting stories Eli told – about how God had chosen the people of Israel to be his own special people. How he had rescued them from Egypt. How he had led them across the River Jordan and given them a land of their own.

Eli showed Samuel God's tent and taught him the rules God had given his people.

Samuel listened and learned.

Once a year Hannah came to see him and bring him new clothes. He looked forward to the visit. But he wasn't really homesick. And Hannah had three more

boys and two girls, so she was much too busy to be sad that Samuel wasn't at home.

One night, when Samuel was asleep in God's tent, a voice woke him up. He thought Eli was calling him, so he ran to the old man's room.

'I heard you call,' he said. 'Did you want something?'

'No,' said Eli. 'I didn't call you. Go back to bed.'

A second time, in the dark, Samuel heard a voice calling him. He ran to Eli again.

'I'm here,' he said. 'You *did* call me.'

'No,' said Eli. 'I didn't call. Go back to bed.'

A third time Samuel heard the voice, got up and went to Eli's room. This time Eli knew that God must have a special message for Samuel.

'Go back to bed,' Eli said. 'And next time you hear the voice, say, "Speak to me, Lord. I'm listening."'

So Samuel went back to bed. And God called him again: 'Samuel! Samuel!'

This time Samuel answered, 'Speak to me, Lord. I'm listening.'

'Give Eli this message,' God said. 'His sons do not love or respect me. Tell Eli they will not be allowed to serve me when he dies.'

When Samuel got up next morning he didn't want to tell Eli what God had said. But Eli made him. The old man listened in silence.

'He is God,' Eli said. 'He will do whatever seems best to him.'

God had chosen Samuel to serve him. As Samuel grew up, God often spoke to him, with a message for his people. And when Samuel spoke, all Israel listened.

Saul and the Lost Donkeys

When Samuel was an old man the people of Israel came to him and said, 'We want a king, like all the other nations.'

Samuel did not think this was a good idea at all. 'If you have a king,' he said, 'he will take your sons to serve in his army, and you will be his slaves.'

But the people would not be put off. They still wanted a king. So God said to Samuel, 'Do what they want. Give them a king.'

Just about that time a man called Kish lost some donkeys. He sent his son Saul to look for them. Saul was young and handsome and a head taller than anyone else. He hunted high and low for his father's missing donkeys, but they were nowhere to be found. His food ran out and he was just about to give up and go home when someone said to him: 'Samuel is wiser than anyone in Israel. Why don't you ask him if he knows where they are?'

So Saul went to find Samuel.

And as soon as Samuel saw him he knew that Saul was the man God had chosen to be king.

'Come and have dinner with me,' Samuel said. 'There's no need to worry about the donkeys. They are quite safe.'

So Saul sat down to dinner with Samuel and thirty other guests. To his great surprise, Samuel treated him as the guest of honour.

Saul spent the night at Samuel's house. Early the next morning he set off for home. Samuel went with him to the outskirts of the town. Then Saul had another surprise. Samuel took a jar of oil and poured it on Saul's head.

'This is the sign that God has chosen you as king to rule his people,' Samuel said. 'And by the way, about those donkeys. When you get home you'll find them there already. Your father's beginning to wonder what's happened to *you*!'

Saul went home. Everything was just as Samuel said. But he told no one that God had chosen him to be king.

Some time later, Samuel called all the people together. 'God says, "I am your God – the one who always comes to your rescue. But you have asked for a king. Very well. Let each tribe gather before me and I will choose your king."'

One by one the tribes came forward. And God chose the tribe of Benjamin.

One by one the families of Benjamin came forward and God chose the family of Matri.

One by one the men of the family of Matri came forward – and God chose Saul, the son of Kish.

But no one could find him!

'He's over there, hiding behind the baggage,' God said. So they ran and brought him out.

Saul was young and handsome and a head taller than anyone else.

'Here is the man God has chosen,' Samuel said. 'There is no one else like him.'

And all the people shouted, 'Long live the king!'

David, the Giant-killer

King Saul and the Israelites were at war with the Philistines. King Saul was a tall man; but Goliath, the Philistine champion, was a giant – almost nine feet tall! He wore a great bronze helmet and carried a huge spear. A soldier walked in front of him carrying his heavy shield.

Every day, morning and night, for forty days Goliath walked up and down in front of the Israelite army.

'I dare one of you to come out and fight me,' he roared. 'If he wins, we will be your slaves. But if I win, you will be our slaves.'

King Saul and his soldiers just stood there. They were all too frightened to fight.

Then one day young David arrived with some food for his soldier-brothers. He was just a shepherd-boy. David listened to Goliath's jeering words. Wasn't anyone going to fight him?

King Saul had offered a huge reward to the man who killed Goliath. 'He shall marry my daughter the princess. And I will let his family off all their taxes.' But no one came forward.

'Who is this Philistine to defy the army of the living God?' David said. His brothers tried to shut him up. Who did he think he was?

But someone told the king and he sent for David.

'Your Majesty,' David said, 'no one should be afraid of this Philistine. I will go and fight him.'

'How could you fight him?' Saul said. 'You are only a baby and he has been a soldier all his life.'

'I've killed lions and bears,' David said, 'when I looked after the sheep. If God can save me from lions and bears he will save me from Goliath.'

'Very well,' said Saul. 'But you must wear my helmet and coat of mail.'

David put it on, but he could hardly walk in it.

'I can't fight like this,' he said. So he took it all off, picked up his shepherd's stick and chose five smooth round stones from the stream for his sling.

Then he went out to meet Goliath.

When Goliath saw David coming he threw back his head and roared with laughter. 'Is this the best the Israelites can do? What's the stick for, boy? Do you think I'm a dog?'

'You have come out to fight with your sword and spear,' David said. 'But I come in the name of the living God. He doesn't need swords and spears to save his people. Soon everyone will know that Israel has a God.'

He ran towards Goliath, letting fly with his sling. The stone smashed into the giant's forehead and knocked him down. He crashed to the ground. Quick as lightning David ran to him, drew Goliath's sword and cut off his head.

There was a great gasp from the Philistine army. Then they turned and ran, with the Israelites in hot pursuit.

God had come to the rescue. His people were safe – thanks to the shepherd-boy who dared to trust him.

The Outlaw

After the fight with Goliath David was a hero. He married princess Michal and went to live at the king's palace. He became a fine soldier and led the army of Israel into battle. Everyone sang his praises.

'They'll be making him king next,' Saul thought. He was jealous and afraid. He wanted to get rid of David.

David was great friends with the king's son, Jonathan. And when Jonathan heard that the king was planning to kill David he went to warn him.

'David has done nothing wrong,' he said to his father. 'He risked his life fighting Goliath. Why do you want to kill him?'

Saul felt ashamed. He promised not to harm David, and for a time all went well. Then one day, when David was playing his harp, the king hurled a spear straight at him. David dodged and managed to escape. But his life was in danger. That night Saul's men kept watch outside David's house.

'If you don't get away tonight they will kill you,' Michal said.

So while it was dark David climbed down from the

window and escaped. Michal wrapped a statue in David's clothes and placed it on the bed. When Saul's men came next morning she told them David was ill. They did not discover till later how she had tricked them. And by that time David was miles away.

David arranged a secret meeting with Jonathan. 'Find out if it's safe for me to come back,' he said.

Then he hid in the fields while Jonathan went to the palace. There was a special feast that day and everyone was there. But David's place was empty.

'Why isn't David here?' asked the king.

'He wanted to go to Bethlehem to see his family,' Jonathan said.

King Saul was furious. 'Why do you always take his side? You will never be king while David lives. Bring him here. He must die.'

'Why? What has he done?' Jonathan asked. But instead of an answer the king seized his spear and hurled it straight at Jonathan.

Next morning Jonathan went out into the fields. He took his bow and arrows, as if he was going for practice. There he met David as planned and told him all that had happened.

'You must go,' Jonathan said. 'From now on you will always be in danger. My father won't rest until you're dead. But I will always be your friend. May God go with you.'

The two friends hugged one another hard and said goodbye. The tears ran down their cheeks. Sadly, Jonathan returned to the palace.

David was an outlaw now, on the run.

A New King

David gathered together a band of outlaws. They were always on the move. And they had some narrow escapes. Often the king's men were close behind.

Once the king himself came right to the mouth of the cave where David and his men were hiding!

Another time David and one of his men crept into Saul's camp at night. The king was asleep, with his spear at his head and a water-jar at his side. David could easily have killed him. But he would not do it.

'God made him king,' David said. 'It's not for me to kill him, no matter what he does.'

Instead, they stole the spear and the water-jar from Saul's side, and slipped away.

When they reached the other side of the valley David shouted across to Saul's men, 'Do you call yourselves guards? What a way to look after the king. Someone came into your camp just now. He could have been killed!'

Saul knew that voice. 'David, is that you?' He felt for his spear. It was gone. Then Saul was dreadfully ashamed. David had spared his life – David, the man he was hunting to kill; David, who had done nothing wrong.

'David, my son, I will never harm you again,' he said. And for a time David was left in peace.

The Philistines heard that David was in disgrace. He was no longer leading the army. Now was the time to attack. There was a great battle, up in the mountains. The Israelites were beaten. Saul and Jonathan were killed.

David became the new king. God had chosen him to take Saul's place. His days as an outlaw were past. Now he was the soldier-king, driving out the enemy nations – north, south, east and west.

In the middle of the land stood the fortress of Jerusalem. It was still in enemy hands. Time and time again the Israelites had tried to storm the city. They

always failed. But this time David had a different plan.

No one could break down the city's strong walls. But there was another way to get inside. An underground tunnel took water into the city, and David discovered the entrance. His men crept up the tunnel and attacked the city from inside.

This time they succeeded. Jerusalem was David's city, the new capital of Israel.

David wanted to make it God's city too. He brought the ark of God's covenant to Jerusalem – that very special box which held the copy of God's laws.

There was great singing and dancing in the streets that day! The king himself led the procession. God was here, with his people – in Jerusalem.

David's great dream was to build God a temple – the most beautiful temple ever – in the city of Jerusalem. But it had to wait till the wars were over. Meantime there was work for a soldier to do. With his army David turned the struggling little kingdom of Israel into a mighty land. He drove out the Philistines once and for all. He made the frontiers strong. At last there was peace.

Solomon
Makes his Choice

Never before or since has there been a king like David. He was a great soldier; but there have been other soldier-kings. He made wonderful music and wrote beautiful poems; other kings have done that too. But David was a man after God's own heart. He loved God and he trusted him – all his life long.

David wasn't a goodie-goodie. He did some very wrong things. He even fixed it for one of his generals to die in battle, so that David could marry his beautiful wife Bathsheba. But when David did something wrong and God told him about it, he was *really* sorry, and he tried his hardest to put things right.

God loved David. He promised to make him the first of a line of kings that would go on for ever. When David was old he gave the kingdom to his son Solomon. The trumpets blew. 'Long live King Solomon,' everyone shouted.

'Be sure to do all that God tells you,' David said to his son. 'And you must build God's temple, here in Jerusalem. Everything is ready.'

David died and Solomon became king.

One night he had a dream. In his dream God said, 'You may choose one special gift. What is it to be?'

'I want to be a good king, like my father,' Solomon said. 'But I'm young and have a lot to learn. So I choose wisdom. That's the gift I need to rule your people well.'

God was pleased.

'I *will* make you wise,' he said, 'wiser than anyone has ever been before or will ever be. I will also give you riches and honour. And if you obey me as your father did you will have a long life too.'

When he woke up, Solomon knew it wasn't just a dream. God really had promised to make him wise.

One day two women came to him.

'We live in the same house,' the first one said. 'And we were both expecting babies. I had a lovely baby boy. Two days later that woman had a baby too. But her baby died in the night. And while I was asleep she stole my baby and put her dead baby in the bed with me.'

'It's a lie,' the second woman said. 'The baby's mine.'

What was King Solomon to do? How could he find out who was telling the truth?

'Each of you says the baby is hers,' he said. 'Very well.' And he called to one of the guards.

'Draw your sword and cut the child in two,' he said. 'Let each of the women have half.' (He was testing them.)

The real mother cried out in dismay, 'Please don't kill him! Please, your Majesty! Let her have the child.'

But the other woman said, 'Go ahead, cut the child in two. Then neither of us will have him.'

Then Solomon said, 'Don't kill the baby. Give him to
the first woman. She loves the child. She is the real
mother.'

Everyone was amazed at Solomon's wisdom. His
fame spread far and wide.

A Queen Comes Visiting

King Solomon did as his father said. He built a wonderful temple in Jerusalem – a house for God. It was made of stone and lined with cedar, carved with fruit and flowers. The temple had two rooms, like God's tent in the desert. They put the ark of God's covenant in the private inner room. Above it were two huge winged beasts, carved from wood and covered in gold. The inside of the temple was covered all over with beaten gold – even the floor. Solomon used the finest craftsmen.

The temple took seven years to build. When it was finished, they held a great celebration. The priests were put in charge of the temple, to take care of it, to arrange the music and the services, the festivals and sacrifices.

Solomon built himself a fine palace with a splendid throne-room. He built a palace for his queen, the king of Egypt's daughter. He built fortress cities too, outside Jerusalem.

He was a great king and his fame spread. He was wiser than the wise men of the East. He wrote proverbs and songs. He was rich. Great men from many lands came to his court.

Far away, across the desert, tales of Solomon's wealth and wisdom reached the Queen of Sheba. She made up her mind to visit King Solomon and see for herself if the stories she had heard were true.

So she set out across the desert with all her attendants, and camels loaded with spices and jewels and gold. As she journeyed she made a list of all the hardest questions she could think of, to test the king.

The Queen of Sheba met King Solomon. She asked him all her questions. And he answered every one – even the hardest. She saw his new palace and the great feasts he held there. She saw the wonderful temple he had built for God. It took her breath away!

'When I heard all those stories about you,' she said to the king, 'I couldn't believe they were true. But I know now that they didn't tell me even half of it. Your God has made you king and given you all this because of his great love for the people of Israel.'

Then she gave Solomon the gifts she had brought with her – sweet-smelling spices, glowing jewels and gleaming gold.

King Solomon gave the Queen of Sheba presents in return – and everything she asked him for. Then she and her attendants returned to their own land.

Elijah and
the Great Drought

King Solomon was wealthy and famous and wise. But he married many foreign wives. And he began to worship their gods. He did not love and obey God as his father King David had done. And he was hard on his people.

Solomon's son was worse. Ten of the twelve tribes of Israel rebelled. They chose a king of their own. Only the tribes of Judah and Benjamin stayed loyal to the kings of David's family line.

The kings who ruled the ten tribes of Israel did not obey God or follow him. Things went from bad to worse. Ahab became king – and he didn't care about God at all.

But God still cared about his people. He wanted to bring King Ahab to his senses. So he sent Elijah to the king with a message.

'God says, you pay no attention to me, but I am the living God of Israel. I tell you there will be no rain until I give the word.'

The king was not bothered at first. It was always dry in summer. But the autumn came and it did not rain. No rain that winter. No rain the next spring. Then it was summer again; blazing sun, day after day – not a cloud in the sky.

There was no rain – and no water in the rivers and streams. No water to make the new corn grow. No grass for the sheep and cattle. No green anywhere. Just parched dry ground; and dust swirling in the wind; animals dying . . .

Where was Elijah all this time?

He was safe in God's care.

'You must go into hiding,' God said, as Elijah left the palace. 'There's a place near Cherith Brook. You will have water to drink. And I will send the ravens to bring you food.'

Elijah did as God said. He had water from the brook to drink. And every morning and every evening the ravens brought him food.

Then the brook dried up. But Elijah was still safe in God's care.

'Go to the town of Zarephath,' God said to him. 'There's a widow there who will feed you.'

So Elijah went to Zarephath. He found the widow gathering sticks for a fire.

'Please could you give me a drink?' he asked. 'I'm thirsty – and hungry too. Could you let me have some bread?'

'I have no bread left,' she said to him. 'Just a handful of flour and a few drops of oil. I was going to light a fire to cook them for myself and my son: our last meal. When we've eaten that we shall starve to death.'

'Don't worry,' Elijah said. 'You can have your meal. But make me a small loaf first. Then bake what's left for you and your son. For God says, "Your bowl of flour will not run out, your jar of oil will not run dry, before the day that I send rain."'

So the widow did as Elijah said.

There was enough for that day's meal

. . . and the next

. . . and the next

. . . day after day, for many days.

Then the widow knew that Elijah had spoken the truth. She and her son, as well as Elijah, were safe in God's care.

The Dare

Month after month went by and there was no rain. The food was running out. People were hungry. Even King Ahab was worried. There was no food for his horses!

Then God said to Elijah, 'Go and tell the king that I am going to send rain.'

The king frowned when he saw Elijah.

'Here comes trouble,' he growled.

'Not me,' Elijah said. 'You are the cause of all the trouble – because you disobey God and worship Baal. I'll show you who is God. Bring all the people to me on Mount Carmel, and all the prophets of Baal.'

So everyone gathered on Mount Carmel to see what Elijah would do.

'I am the only one of God's prophets left,' Elijah said. 'But there are 450 prophets of Baal. Today we shall see who is the real God. You must choose who to follow – God or Baal.

'We shall need two bulls, one for me and one for the prophets of Baal. We shall each build a fire and cut up a bull and put it on top. But we won't light the fire. Instead we shall pray. I will pray to God. Baal's prophets will pray to him. And the God who sends fire is the real God.'

He turned to the prophets of Baal. 'Your turn first,' he said.

So the prophets of Baal gathered wood and cut up their bull and put it on top. Then they prayed to Baal – all morning. They danced around the pile of wood.

'Answer us, Baal! Answer us, Baal.'

But no answer came.

At midday Elijah began to mock: 'Pray a bit louder! Maybe your god is asleep. Or perhaps he's gone out for the day.'

So the prophets of Baal prayed louder. They gashed themselves with knives till the blood ran. They ranted and raved all afternoon. But still no answer came. No sound was heard.

Then Elijah gathered the people around him. He piled up stones to make an altar. He dug a deep trench all around. He put the wood on the altar, cut up the bull and put the pieces on top.

'Fill four jars with water,' he said to the people. 'And pour it over the meat and the wood.' They did as he said.

'Do it again . . . And again.' The water ran down and filled up the trench.

Then Elijah prayed: 'Lord God, prove now that you are the God of Israel, and that I am your prophet, and that I have done all this at your command. Answer me, Lord. And bring your people back to you.'

Then the fire came.

It burnt the meat on the altar, and the wood and the stones. It scorched the ground and dried up all the water in the trench.

When the people saw it, they threw themselves face down on the ground. 'The Lord is God!' they shouted. 'The Lord alone is God!'

That night, before some of them even got home, the rain came.

'Go and Wash!'

God gave his people another prophet after Elijah. His name was Elisha.

In Syria, the country to the north of Israel, there was a famous general called Naaman. General Naaman led the Syrian army in raids on Israel. Sometimes they carried people off to be their slaves.

That's how one little Israelite girl came to be the servant of General Naaman's wife. And it was lucky for Naaman that she was.

Naaman and his wife were kind, and the little girl grew to love them – though she missed her own family very much.

One day she heard that General Naaman was sick. The servants discussed it in whispers. He didn't have any pain. He wasn't running a temperature. But there were ugly marks on his skin. Naaman had a dreadful disease – he would have to resign from the army, leave home and go away to live all by himself.

'How I wish my master could go to the prophet Elisha,' the little girl said to Naaman's wife. 'I know he could make him well.'

Naaman's wife told her husband; he told the king; and the king wrote a letter.

It was addressed to the king of Israel. And this is what it said: 'The man who brings this letter is General Naaman. I'm sending him to you for a cure.'

When the king of Israel read the letter, he tore his hair! 'Does the king of Syria think I'm God? How am I expected to cure this man?'

But the prophet Elisha heard what had happened and sent word to the king. 'Send Naaman to me.'

So General Naaman drove to Elisha's house. But Elisha didn't even come to the door. Instead he sent his servant with a message.

'Elisha says you must go and wash seven times in the River Jordan. Then you will be cured.'

General Naaman stormed off in a rage. He'd expected Elisha to say a long prayer and wave his hands about and cure him.

'If I needed a wash, I could have gone to one of our rivers in Syria,' he said.

His servants pleaded with him: 'If Elisha had asked you to do something hard, you would have done it. So why not wash in the river, and be cured?'

So Naaman went down to the river and washed. Not once, not twice, but seven times – just as Elisha had said. And when he came out, he was cured. Not a mark on his skin – anywhere.

'Now I know there is no God but the God of Israel,' Naaman said. And he went back to thank Elisha.

The King
who Was Only Seven

There was mourning in the little southern kingdom of Judah, the part of Israel ruled by kings of David's family line. King Ahaziah was dead. And Athaliah, the king's mother, had gone crazy.

'Now I shall be queen,' she said, when she heard of her son's death. And she gave orders for every single one of the royal family to be killed – all King Ahaziah's children.

Every single one of them died that day – except for the baby, Joash. Somehow, without anyone knowing, his aunt managed to smuggle him out of the palace before the soldiers found him.

She took him to the temple for the priest to take care of. She knew he would be safe there. For six years the secret was kept. No one knew that Joash was alive, except for his aunt, the servant who looked after him, and Jehoiada the priest.

Being shut up in the temple wasn't much fun for a little boy. Joash couldn't go out to play. And when anyone came he had to hide.

The people were very unhappy. Everyone hated the

cruel queen. They thought no one was left to carry on the line of kings which began with King David. But God had promised that the kings of David's family line would rule for ever. It was God who had kept little Joash safe.

When Joash was seven, Jehoiada the priest sent for the officers in charge of the royal guard. They came to the temple.

'I have something to tell you. There is someone you must meet,' Jehoiada said. 'But you must promise to keep the secret.'

The soldiers couldn't imagine what the secret was – but they promised. Then Jehoiada sent for Joash.

Who was this boy, the soldiers wondered? What was he doing in the temple?'

Then Jehoiada explained. He told them how Joash had been saved when the rest of his family were killed.

'Now,' he said, 'listen carefully, while I tell you what to do.'

On the Sabbath day, when the guards came off duty at the palace they went straight to the temple. They stood in front of the temple with swords drawn, ready to kill anyone who came near the new king.

Then Jehoiada led Joash out on to the steps for all the people to see. He placed a crown on his head and a copy of God's laws in his hands. Then he proclaimed Joash king.

'Long live the king! Long live the king!'

The trumpets sounded again and again. The people clapped and shouted in excitement.

Queen Athaliah heard the noise and hurried to the

temple. She saw the young king standing there, with the
soldiers of the guard and all the happy people.

'Treason! Treason!' she shrieked.

But no one paid any attention to her. Then the
guards seized her and took her away.

Joash walked to the palace escorted by the royal
guard. They led him to the throne and he sat down.

Joash was seven years old; and he was king.

Enemy at the Gates

In the royal city of Jerusalem King Hezekiah was getting ready for war. The Assyrians were on the march. There wasn't much time.

'The Assyrian army will need water,' thought the king. 'We must cut off their supply.' So he had all the springs outside the city blocked up. And his workmen dug a tunnel through the solid rock to bring the water inside the city.

The king sent for the builders. 'Repair the walls,' he said. 'Build strong towers – and a brand-new wall outside the old one.'

The king sent for the blacksmiths and leather-workers. 'We need more shields and spears,' he said. 'Start work right away.'

Everyone got busy. Such a banging and a hammering as had never been heard before.

The king spoke to his people. They knew all about the Assyrians. How powerful they were – no one could stop them. How terribly cruel they were, showing no mercy.

'Don't be afraid,' the king said. 'Be strong. We have more power than all the Assyrians put together. They are only men. But we have God to fight for us.'

One by one the cities fell. The Assyrian army came closer and closer, until Jerusalem was surrounded. From the city walls the people could see row upon row of fierce-looking men, armed to the teeth. The soldiers' spears glittered in the sun.

The Assyrian general spoke to the people in their own

language: 'King Hezekiah says your God will save you. But don't you believe him. Did the gods of those other cities save them? We'll stay here until you starve to death.' (He was trying to frighten God's people.)

'Come out and surrender. You are hungry now – and it's going to get worse. If you come out you can eat grapes from your own vines and figs from your own fig-trees and have water to drink from your own wells.'

But the people of Jerusalem did not answer.

King Hezekiah was worried. He sent his chief officials to see God's prophet Isaiah and ask for his advice.

Isaiah listened to all they said and sent back his answer: 'God says, "Don't let the Assyrians frighten you. Don't believe them when they say I cannot save you. Very soon the Emperor of Assyria will hear that there is trouble in his own land, and the army will go home."'

King Hezekiah prayed to God: 'Lord, you are our God. You made the whole world and everything in it. You heard the Assyrians say you could not save us. You know how many nations they have conquered. Lord God, rescue us now. Then they will know that you are the one and only God.'

That night the Emperor had bad news from home. Assyria was under attack.

Next day the Assyrian army marched away.

The people flung open the city gates and came out, singing and dancing for joy.

'Thank you, God,' they said. 'You have saved our lives.'

When No One Would Listen

God saved his people from the Assyrians. But they soon forgot. They disobeyed his laws. They worshipped other gods. The rich grew richer. The poor grew poorer. God's people told lies and cheated – until God could not bear it any longer.

He decided to give them one last chance. He would send Jeremiah with a message. Jeremiah wasn't very old and he was dreadfully shy.

'There's no need to be frightened,' God said. 'I will tell you exactly what to say. And I will take good care of you.'

After that, whenever God gave him something to say Jeremiah just *had* to say it. He didn't want to. He was still shy. But the words came tumbling out. He could not hold them back.

Jeremiah told the people how God hated the wicked things they did. He told them how wrong they were to worship foreign gods. And he begged them to come back to God before it was too late.

At first the people just put their hands over their ears and refused to listen. Then they grew angry.

'God says, if you do not listen to him, if you do not return to him and mend your ways, he will destroy Jerusalem!' said Jeremiah.

When they heard this the people were so angry they almost killed him.

'Traitor! Traitor!' they shouted.

Jeremiah was very afraid. But he went on telling people what God said. He was sent to prison, but even that did not stop him.

God told Jeremiah that the king of Babylon and his army would capture Jerusalem and break down its walls. He would take God's people away to distant lands. But God would bring them back when they had learned their lesson.

One day, when Jeremiah tried to leave Jerusalem to visit his family, he was arrested.

'Deserter!' they said. 'You're leaving us to join the Babylonians.' And Jeremiah was locked up. But he still kept talking.

'God will give this city to the king of Babylon. If you stay here you will starve to death or be killed. Surrender now, and save your lives.'

Jeremiah was thrown into a deep well and left there. There was no water in it, but he was up to his knees in mud. He would have starved to death if Ebedmelech hadn't begged for his release. They hauled him out of the well, just in time.

The day came when all God had said would happen came true. It was the worst day of Jeremiah's life. If only people had listened!

King Nebuchadnezzar of Babylon marched into the

country with his great army. They surrounded the city. For over a year no one could go in or out. The food ran out and the people were starving. Then the Babylonians battered down the city wall. They destroyed the king's palace and took him prisoner. They destroyed God's temple. The proud city of Jerusalem was in ruins, and the people of God were taken away to distant lands.

Now at last they were glad to listen.

'Don't be afraid,' Jeremiah said. 'God says "I will come and save you. I will bring my people home again." And that's a promise.'

The Men who Walked Through Fire

Back home in Babylon King Nebuchadnezzar decided to give some of his prisoners special training. That was how Daniel and his three friends – Shadrach, Meshach and Abednego – came to be at court. Daniel's best subject was dreams and visions, and what they meant.

One night the king had a dream. It worried him so much he couldn't sleep. Next morning he sent for his wise men.

'Tell me what it means,' he ordered.

'Just tell us what it was and we'll explain,' they said.

'No,' said the king. 'You tell *me* – or I'll have you torn limb from limb!'

When Daniel and his friends heard what had happened they asked God to help them. And God told Daniel the dream and what it meant.

Daniel went to the king.

'Only God can tell you your dream,' he said. 'It's about what will happen in the future.' And he explained it all.

The great King Nebuchadnezzar bowed low.

'Your God is the greatest of all gods,' he said. And he made Daniel his chief adviser.

Some time later the king ordered his men to set up a huge golden statue of one of his gods.

When it was ready, he ordered everyone to come and see it.

'My musicians will play,' said the king, 'and when the music starts *everyone* must bow down and worship. Anyone who disobeys will be flung into the fiery furnace.'

The music began and everyone bowed low – all except Shadrach, Meshach and Abednego. (Daniel was away on the king's business.)

The Babylonians rushed to tell the king, and King Nebuchadnezzar exploded with rage.

'Is it true that you refuse to worship my god and bow down to his statue?' he roared. 'I'll have you thrown into the fiery furnace.'

'Our God can save us, even from the fiery furnace, if he wants to,' the three men said. 'But in any case we cannot worship your god or bow down to his statue.'

King Nebuchadnezzar went red in the face. 'Heat the furnace seven times hotter!'

Shadrach, Meshach and Abednego were tied hand

and foot and thrown into the white-hot centre of the fiery furnace.

Then the king rubbed his eyes. He couldn't believe it. There were *four* men in the fire, walking about. And the fourth one – the king trembled – the fourth one looked like a god!

King Nebuchadnezzar went to the door of the fiery furnace. He called to the three friends.

'Shadrach! Meshach! Abednego! Servants of the most high God. Come out!'

They came out. Their clothes were not burned. Not one hair was singed.

'Their God sent his angel to rescue them,' said the king, 'because they would not worship any god but him. No other god could have done that.'

He turned to his people. 'If anyone says anything against the God of Shadrach, Meshach and Abednego,' he roared, 'I'll have him torn limb from limb!'

Thrown to the Lions

The years went by. Babylon fell to the Medes and Persians. And Darius became king. He had to choose a new government. And he decided to make Daniel Prime Minister.

The other officials were jealous. They wanted to get rid of Daniel. If only he weren't so good and honest and loyal to the king!

Then they hit on a plan.

Three times every day Daniel went upstairs to a room in his house which had a window facing Jerusalem; there he knelt down and prayed to God. (Daniel had lived in Jerusalem before King Nebuchadnezzar took him prisoner.) Daniel's enemies knew that nothing would stop him praying to his God. So they went to see the king.

'O King, live for ever!' they said. 'We have all agreed on a new law. For thirty days no one may ask anything from any god or man except from your Majesty. If anyone disobeys he'll be thrown to the lions! Would you sign here, please?'

King Darius signed the order.

Daniel heard about the new law. He knew that his life

was in danger. But still he went upstairs as usual, three times a day, and knelt at the window and prayed to God.

As soon as they saw him his enemies went to the king.

'O King, live for ever! That order you gave. Daniel has disobeyed it. He prays to his God three times a day, for everyone to see.'

The king was most upset when he heard this. He didn't want to have Daniel thrown to the lions. But the Prime Minister couldn't be allowed to break the law. And the king's word can never be changed. So Daniel was arrested.

'May your God, whom you serve so faithfully, rescue you,' said the king – though he really didn't have much hope.

Daniel was thrown into the lion-pit and the entrance stone was sealed with the king's seal. Darius was very unhappy. There was no music or dancing at the palace that night. The king couldn't eat. He didn't sleep a wink.

As soon as it was light he hurried to the lion-pit and called out in a very worried voice: 'Daniel, servant of the living God. Was your God able to save you from the lions?' He didn't expect to hear an answer. He was sure the lions had eaten Daniel for supper.

But Daniel answered, 'O King, live for ever! God closed the jaws of the lions so that none of them hurt me. He knew that I had done nothing wrong.'

The king was overjoyed. He gave orders for Daniel to be pulled out of the lion-pit. Everyone could see he wasn't hurt at all – because he trusted God.

The king had all Daniel's enemies thrown to the lions for breakfast. And that was the last of them.

Then he wrote to all his subjects: 'It is my command that everyone in my great Empire should fear and respect Daniel's God. He is the living God. He saved Daniel from being eaten by the lions. He is God for ever.'

Swallowed Alive!

Once upon a time there was a man called Jonah. One day God said to him, 'Jonah, I want you to go to Nineveh with a message. You're to tell the people there that I've seen the wicked and cruel things they do – and unless they mend their ways I shall destroy the city.'

But Jonah didn't do as God said. Instead he decided he'd run away to sea. He was just in time to catch a boat for Spain. God won't find me there, he thought.

But when the boat was out at sea there was a terrible storm. The wind blew a gale. The waves broke over the side and the boat began to sink.

The sailors fell on their knees and prayed to their gods. But Jonah, who had gone below, slept through it all – until the captain woke him up!

'Get up! Pray to your god for help!' he said. 'Maybe he'll spare our lives.'

'Something must have made God angry,' the sailors said. 'That's why he's sent this storm. Maybe it's one of us.' So they tossed up to see who it was.

'Jonah! You're the one,' they said. 'You must have done something dreadful!'

Then Jonah told them he was running away from God. 'Throw me overboard,' he said. 'It's all my fault.'

They didn't want to, but the storm got worse. So they said a prayer – and threw Jonah overboard. At once the wind dropped and the sea grew calm. The sailors were impressed by Jonah's God.

God had no intention of letting Jonah drown. He sent a huge fish that swallowed Jonah alive, just when he thought his last moment had come.

It wasn't very nice in the stomach of the fish. It was dark and smelly. But Jonah was so glad to be alive he prayed to God, right there.

'I thought I was going to drown,' he said. 'But you saved my life. I'm sorry I ran away. And I promise to do whatever you say in future.'

Then God had a word with the fish – and the fish spat Jonah up on to the beach.

God said to Jonah for the second time, 'I want you to go to Nineveh with a message.' This time Jonah went. He walked through the city for three whole days telling everyone what God had said: 'In forty days Nineveh will be destroyed.'

The people of Nineveh listened; they were so sorry for the wicked and cruel things they had done that the king and the people mended their ways. And God spared the city.

But Jonah was very fed up. He felt that God had made him look silly. 'In forty days Nineveh will be destroyed,' he had said. And then nothing had happened! Besides, the people of Nineveh were so wicked they deserved to die. Jonah sat outside the city in the burning sun and sulked.

'Jonah!' God said. 'Why are you so angry?'

'You know why!' Jonah said, rather rudely. 'I thought all the time that you wouldn't do it. You are too loving and patient and kind. That's why I ran away to Spain.'

'I made those people,' God said. 'Why should I want to destroy them? Isn't it far better they should mend their ways?'

'Oh, I suppose so,' Jonah said, grudgingly. Then he smiled. 'Yes, of course it is,' he said.

Home to Jerusalem!

When God makes a promise he always keeps it. God had promised to bring his people home from the lands of exile. He promised that Jerusalem would be built again – when his people had learned their lesson.

And they really had. They listened to him now. They kept his laws. They were loyal to him. So God kept his promise.

King Cyrus of Persia issued a proclamation. It was read aloud for everyone to hear.

'Let all my people hear the king's command. I, Cyrus, whom God has made ruler of Persia, command that God's people return to Jerusalem. Let them re-build God's temple. I hereby return all the gold and silver cups and bowls which King Nebuchadnezzar took from God's temple and brought to Babylon.'

What wonderful news! The Jews – as God's people were called in Persia – could hardly believe their ears. They were going home – at last!

It was a long and dangerous journey; 800 miles across the desert and over the mountains. They would have to walk all the way. But who cared? They must get ready. They must pack.

King Cyrus ordered his people to help, and the presents poured in. Gold and silver, food for the journey, beautiful things for the temple of God.

Everyone was so excited when they started out.

But when they got to Jerusalem the grown-ups cried. It was just a tumbledown ruin. There was no sign of the temple. The great city walls were all broken down and blackened by fire. Other people had settled in the land while they had been away.

But after a good night's sleep everyone felt more cheerful. First they must find somewhere to live. Then they would start work on the temple.

The new temple wasn't as grand as the one King Solomon had built. And the work took a very long time. But it was done at last. There were services again, and music and festivals.

But Jerusalem wouldn't be a city until its walls were rebuilt. In those days every city had strong walls all around it. If an enemy came, the gates could be shut and barred and the people inside were safe.

Nehemiah had stayed behind in Persia when the rest of his people left for home. But when he heard that

Jerusalem was still in ruins he asked the king to let him go and help. He was an important man, the taster of the king's own wine.

When he reached Jerusalem he took a good look around, on his own. Then he came up with a plan. Each family was given part of the wall to work on. The people who lived inside the city worked on the bit of wall nearest to their own houses.

So all around the city the walls began to grow – little by little, higher and higher.

The foreign settlers didn't like this at all. They tried to make them stop building. But Nehemiah gave everyone weapons and they went on building – with swords

strapped to their waists; a weapon in one hand and a pick or trowel in the other. While half of them worked on the building, half stood guard.

'If the bugle sounds, gather around me,' said Nehemiah. 'But don't worry. God will fight for us.'

Every day they worked, from the minute it was light until the stars came out at night. The walls grew higher and higher.

Nehemiah was a good leader. And he didn't forget to pray. He prayed when his enemies tried to scare him: 'Please God, make me strong.'

In fifty-two days, with God's help, the walls were finished. Jerusalem was a city again. The temple was rebuilt. God's people were home again!

They marched in a great procession all around the city, on top of the wall. The priests blew their trumpets. The cymbals crashed. Harps played. The people sang at the tops of their voices. They were all giving thanks to God. He had kept his promise.

Stories from
THE NEW
TESTAMENT

God's plan to save the spoiled world
by sending a very special person –
the story of Jesus

A Very Special Baby

In the courtyard of a little house in Nazareth a girl called Mary was kneading dough for the day's baking. Mary was engaged to Joseph, the village carpenter, and she was thinking about the wedding. Not long now.

The sun was so bright when she looked up that she didn't notice the stranger at first. Then he spoke.

'Mary! I have a message for you from God. The time has come for him to send his Son into the world – the King he promised so long ago. And he has chosen you to be the mother of this very special baby. You are to call him Jesus.'

Mary was longing to ask questions. But she felt a little afraid of the awesome angel messenger. So she simply said: 'I am willing to do whatever God wants.'

Nine months later, when the baby was almost due, Mary and Joseph set out on the long journey south to Bethlehem. At that time the land of Israel belonged to the Roman Empire. And the Emperor wanted a new list of all his people, to make sure they paid their taxes. So everyone had to return to their home town. Joseph's family were descendants of King David; they came from Bethlehem.

Eighty long miles Mary and Joseph walked, with the donkey to carry their food – and clothes for the baby. Mary was tired out when they got there. But Bethlehem was crowded with visitors and there was nowhere for them to stay. Mary could feel the pains that meant her baby was coming. Then at last the innkeeper took pity on her. The place was full, but they could spend the night where the animals were.

Out on the hills the shepherds wrapped their cloaks around them and drew close to the fire as they kept watch over the sleeping sheep. The stars had never seemed so bright. Brighter and brighter. Dazzling. Then, out of the brightness, came the voice of an angel.

'Good news,' the angel said. 'Great joy for everyone. God's Saviour – Christ the Lord – has been born in

Bethlehem today. You will find him in a manger at the inn.'

Then the shepherds heard the singing: music that seemed to come from heaven itself.

'Glory to God,' a thousand angel voices sang, 'and peace to everyone on earth.'

'Let's go to Bethlehem and see,' the shepherds said to one another as the singing died away. So they made the sheep safe and hurried over the hills.

There they found Mary and Joseph, just as the angel said. And the very special baby, tightly wrapped and lying in a manger.

Follow That Star!

Away in the East lived men who studied the stars. One night they noticed a bright new star in the sky.

'Whatever can this mean?' they said, and hurried to consult their books.

'It means a baby's been born who'll be king of the Jews,' one of them said. 'We must go and pay our respects.'

Next morning they packed their bags and saddled their camels, ready to set off across the desert. Each of them chose a special present for the baby king. They journeyed by night, following the star. When the sun came up and the stars faded, they camped, resting through the long hot day.

At last they came to Jerusalem, capital of the Jewish kingdom. They made their way to the palace and asked to see the king. But there was no new royal baby there – and King Herod was worried by this talk of a new king.

He called his advisers.

'Where do the prophets say God's promised King will be born?' he asked them.

'In Bethlehem,' they answered.

So King Herod sent his visitors to Bethlehem.

'When you find the new king, be sure to come back and tell me. I want to pay my respects too.' (He didn't, of course. He wanted to kill the baby.)

The star led the visitors all the way.

Mary and Joseph were amazed when these tall, bearded strangers on camels stopped at the door of the little house where they were staying. The men came in and knelt before the baby.

Then they unwrapped their presents.

Gold, the proper present for a king.

Frankincense, the present people gave to God.

And myrrh, the ointment used at funerals.

When she saw this Mary shivered and hugged her baby close. What could it mean?

The visitors did not report to King Herod. God warned them in a dream, and they went home another way.

Then God told Joseph he must leave Bethlehem. King Herod would be looking for the baby to kill him. So the little family, with the donkey to carry their things, set out once again. This time they went further south, across the border into Egypt.

When King Herod realized the visitors had tricked him he was beside himself with rage.

'Go to Bethlehem,' he ordered his soldiers. 'And kill every baby boy under two.' They did as he said. But the baby Herod wanted had gone.

Mary and Joseph and Jesus stayed in Egypt until King Herod died. Then they went home to the carpenter's shop in Nazareth.

Jesus Grows Up

Jesus loved the smell of wood as Joseph worked. He trickled the sawdust and shavings through his fingers. He begged Joseph to let him help. And as soon as he was old enough Joseph taught him how to use the carpenter's tools.

Soon he was old enough to go with the other boys to the synagogue school. He learned by heart the laws God gave his people. He loved the teacher's stories – about Abraham and Joseph and Moses. He was eager to learn the history of his people – the stories of King David, the building of God's temple, and the terrible years of exile.

Jesus heard how the Jewish people had come home to the land of Israel and built the temple again. But they weren't free for long. Soon the Roman army came and Israel became part of the great Roman Empire. There were soldiers everywhere in Jesus' day. The Jewish people hated them.

But the teacher said that God had promised to send his people a new king.

'He will set us free – and send the Romans packing.'

*

By the time Jesus was twelve he felt almost grown up. Next birthday he would count as a man in the synagogue. He would join in the Sabbath meetings for prayer and hear God's law read and explained. It was very exciting!

Joseph and Mary had promised, this time, to take him with them when they went to Jerusalem for the Passover Festival. Jesus counted the days!

At last they were packed and ready to go – with a noisy, laughing crowd of friends who lived near. It would take several days to get there, so there was all the excitement of camping on the way.

Jesus never forgot his first sight of Jerusalem – the great walls, golden in the sunshine, and the shining temple. They all sang as they toiled up the hill to the city gates, tiredness forgotten.

Every year at the Passover Festival the Jews remembered how, long ago, God had rescued them from being slaves in Egypt. Every family killed and roasted a lamb, as they had on that terrible night when death came to all the first-born sons of Egypt but 'passed over' God's people.

The visitors from Nazareth stayed a week, then they set out for home. Mary thought Jesus was with Joseph. Joseph thought he was with the other boys. So no one noticed he was missing until they stopped to camp for the night.

Mary and Joseph felt sick with worry. Whatever could have happened to him? As soon as it was light they started back, asking everyone they met if they had seen a boy on his own.

They found him at last in the courtyards of the temple, listening to the teachers and asking questions. He was quite calm and looked puzzled when he saw their anxious faces.

'But surely you knew I had to be in my Father's house,' he said. (He was talking about God.)

Mary and Joseph simply could not understand it. So they took him home, where he was the same loving, obedient boy he had always been.

Testing! Testing!

John was born in the same year as Jesus. He was a special baby too. He came when his mother and father were much too old to have children. But God had a special job for John to do.

When he was grown up John began to tell everyone God's message.

'Good news,' he said. 'God's promised King is coming soon. We must all get ready. We must give up our bad old ways and make a new start. Be baptized and God will forgive you.'

Crowds came to John the Baptist. They confessed the wrong things they had done and he took them down into the River Jordan, as a sign that their sins were washed away.

One day Jesus joined the crowd. When his turn came, John tried to make him change his mind.

'You don't need to be baptized,' he protested. 'You've not done anything wrong. You should be the one baptizing me!'

But Jesus insisted. And as he came up out of the water, John saw God's Holy Spirit alight like a dove on Jesus' shoulder. Then he heard God's voice, saying: 'This is my own dear Son.'

After that, Jesus spent forty days alone in the desert. He knew that his time as a carpenter was over. God had other work for him to do. So he needed to be alone with God to pray.

There was no food in the desert and Jesus grew very hungry. That was when the testing began. Just as the first woman, in the garden of Eden, heard the voice of the snake tempting her to disobey God, so now Jesus heard the tempter's voice.

'If you are God's Son, order these stones to turn into bread.'

Jesus could have done it. But he knew it was wrong to use his special power for himself. So he answered in the Bible's words: 'Bread is not enough to live on. We need God's message too.'

Then the tempter took Jesus to the topmost point of the temple in Jerusalem.

'If you are God's Son,' he said, 'prove it. Throw yourself down. God will send his angels to save you.'

Again Jesus answered in the Bible's words: 'Don't you know that we must not put God to the test?'

The tempter tried again. He took Jesus to a high mountain and showed him all the kingdoms of the world.

'I will give you all this,' he said, 'if only you will serve me.'

'Go away, Satan,' Jesus said. 'The Bible tells us we must love God and serve no one but him.'

Then, at last, the tempter went away. But he had not given up.

Friends of the Teacher

After the testing Jesus went home to Nazareth. On the Sabbath – the Jewish day of rest, like Sunday – he went to the synagogue as usual. He stood up and read these words from the Bible:

'God's Spirit is upon me. He has chosen me to bring good news to the poor, to set the prisoners free, and give sight to the blind.'

Everyone was quiet as Jesus sat down and began to explain.

'The words of the prophet Isaiah have come true today,' he said.

From that time on, Jesus became a teacher, going from village to village telling everyone God's good news. And it wasn't just words. He *proved* that God had given him special power. Everywhere he went he made sick people well.

He left Nazareth and made his home in a little town on the shore of Lake Galilee. He often watched the fishermen set out in their boats at night, returning in the early morning with their catch.

One day, as he stood on the beach with people crowding round, he saw two boats lying there. The fishermen were washing their nets. So Jesus got into Peter's boat and asked him to push it into the water, so that he could speak to the people from there.

Afterwards he said to Peter: 'Go out a bit further and let down the nets for a catch.'

'Night is the best time for fishing,' Peter said. But he did as Jesus told him. And there were so many fish the nets nearly broke. The men in the other boat came to help, and both boats were so full of fish they almost sank.

It was then that Peter realized Jesus was someone very special.

'Leave your fishing,' Jesus said to him. 'Come with me – and catch people instead!' All four fishermen – Peter and his brother Andrew, hot-tempered James and his brother John – became friends of the Teacher that day. They went everywhere with him, and soon they were joined by others.

Jesus made friends with all kinds of people. They didn't have to be rich or clever or pretty. He chose twelve of them to be his special friends.

There were the four fishermen.

There was Matthew. He had collected taxes for the Romans before he met Jesus. So no one liked him. Everyone was shocked when Jesus chose Matthew as his friend. But Jesus did not care.

And there was Simon the rebel. He was a fighter, working with the Jews to drive out the Romans.

The others were Philip and Bartholomew, Thomas (the twin), James and Thaddaeus, and Judas – the friend who turned traitor.

The Teacher Says . . .

All through the long hot summer days in Israel people lived out of doors. So when Jesus wanted to teach he didn't go into a school or a church. He held his lessons in the open air.

One place they all liked was up on the hill, overlooking the lake. In the spring the hill was bright with wild flowers, red and yellow and gold. Little flocks of sheep

and goats wandered about, nibbling the grass, under the watchful eye of their shepherd.

Jesus went there one day with a great crowd of people. He found a smooth rock to sit on and his friends gathered close, with the crowd sitting on the grass all around. Then he began to talk.

'I'll tell you a secret,' he said. 'You think you can only be happy if you are rich, or famous, or beautiful. But you're wrong! It's loving God and doing what he wants that makes a person happy. That's the secret. If you love God you can be happy even if you are poor or sick, or someone hurts you.

'God wants you to shine like lights in the world for everyone to see. Then when you are good and kind they will know you are doing as he says, and thank him for it.'

One of Jesus' friends asked him to teach them to pray. They knew he often got up very early to pray – so it must be important.

'God loves you like a father,' Jesus said. 'He wants to talk to you, and he wants you to talk to him. Pray like this.' And he taught them 'the Lord's prayer':

'Our Father in heaven:
May people everywhere respect your holy name;
may your Kingdom come;

may your will be done on earth as it is in heaven.
Give us today the food we need.
Forgive us the wrongs we have done, as we forgive the
wrongs that others have done to us.
Do not bring us to hard testing,
but keep us safe from the Evil One.'
Just then a flock of birds flew low overhead. Jesus
looked at the worried faces of the grown-ups all around
him.

'There's a lesson for you,' he said. 'Look at those
birds. They don't plough and plant and harvest their
food. They don't have a care in the world. But God
looks after them. And look at these flowers. They don't
worry about clothes. Yet God gives them clothes more
beautiful than all King Solomon's wealth could buy. So
don't worry about food and clothes. God loves you
much more than he does the birds and flowers. Just
make up your minds to please him – and he will give you
all you need.'

When lessons were over for the day, Jesus told a
story.

'Two men decided to build,' Jesus said. 'The wise
man built his house on rock. The rain poured down.
The floods came. The wind blew hard. But his house
stood firm because it was built on rock. If you listen,
and do as I say, you are the wise man.

'The silly man built his house on sand. It was easier
to dig and he finished much quicker. But when the rain
poured down and the floods came and the winds blew
hard, the silly man's house fell down. If you listen, but
don't do as I say, you are just as silly as he was.'

The Day of the Storm

One evening Jesus and his friends set out in a boat to cross the lake. Lake Galilee was so big it was almost a sea. It was a lovely lake, with woods and hills all around. All summer long, in the daytime, it sparkled blue beneath the clear blue sky. In the evening the water changed to a pale gold in the light of the setting sun.

It was good to leave the crowds behind and sail away across the still water in that golden evening light. Jesus was so tired he fell fast asleep, his head on a pillow. The others spoke quietly so that they would not disturb him.

Then all of a sudden the wind started to blow, gusting down through the hills and stirring the water. Before long the little boat was tossing and the waves were slap-slapping hard against the side. The sky darkened. The wind blew stronger. And the boat began to pitch. The waves built up so high they started to splash over the side and into the boat.

The sky was so dark now that no one could see the shore. They had to shout above the screaming of the wind. The four fishermen had known many storms on

the lake – but this one made them scared. And there was Jesus, still peacefully sleeping!

It only needed one extra big wave and the boat would fill with water. They would all be drowned!

Someone shook Jesus roughly awake.

'How can you sleep? Don't you care what's happening? Any minute now we shall sink.'

Jesus did not answer. He stood up in the pitching, tossing boat – and spoke to the wind!

'Stop that noise!' he said.

And to the waves, 'Lie down!'

At once the wind died away and there was a great calm.

'Why were you so frightened?' Jesus said to his friends. 'Can't you trust me?'

But they had never felt so afraid – not of the storm now but of this amazing person, who could make even the wind and the waves do as he told them.

The Boy who Shared his Dinner

It was getting late. No one had eaten since breakfast. Everyone was hungry. But where can you get food for 5,000 hungry people, out in the country miles from anywhere?

That morning, Jesus and his friends had decided to take the day off. They had been so very busy lately. So, as the sun came up, they rowed across the lake to find a quiet place on the other side.

But someone saw them go. And soon there were crowds of people running around the lake-shore to be there when the boat landed.

Jesus was tired, but he didn't have the heart to turn them away. Instead he began to talk to them. And when Jesus was talking, no one was ever bored. So it seemed no time at all before the friends of Jesus said: 'It's getting late. It will be dark before long. Send the people away to get something to eat.'

'We can't do that,' said Jesus. 'We must give them something before they go.'

'But where can we get enough food to feed all these

people?' Philip said. 'It will cost a fortune.'

'See what they have,' Jesus said.

No one had anything at all – except one boy. His mother had packed him a picnic: five small loaves and two fish.

He was very hungry. If he shared his dinner there would be nothing left. But he gave it to Jesus all the same.

'Tell everyone to sit down on the grass,' Jesus said.
Then he took the boy's dinner and said grace, thanking
God for the good food he had given them. Jesus broke
the loaves into pieces and divided up the fish. His
friends shared them out.

To their amazement, everyone had more than
enough. When they gathered up the scraps, they filled
twelve baskets!

The boy was so glad he had shared his dinner!

Next day, when the crowd came back, Jesus told them
about another kind of bread.

'I am the living bread,' he said. 'Everyone who
believes in me will be satisfied – not just for one day but
for always.'

'Now I Can See!'

There was a man who had been born blind. He had never seen anyone's face. He had never seen flowers or birds. He lived all his life in the dark – until he met Jesus.

As soon as he saw the man, Jesus went over to speak to him. Then he did a very strange thing. He made a mud pie and put it on the blind man's eyes, and told him to go and wash his face in the Pool of Siloam.

Very surprised, the man went – tap-tapping his way along the street. He washed the mud from his eyes and when he looked up – he could see! He came back along the same street, but now he could see people and houses and green trees. It was wonderful!

Those who lived near knew him at once, but they couldn't believe their eyes.

'Isn't that the blind man who used to sit in the street and beg?' they said. 'No. It can't be. But he looks just like him!'

'Yes. It's me!' said the blind man.

'But what's happened to make you see?'

'It was a man called Jesus,' said the blind man. 'He

put mud on my eyes and told me to wash my face in the Pool of Siloam. So I went and washed – and now I can see!'

You would have thought everyone would be pleased. But some of the religious people – the Pharisees – were angry. No work on the Sabbath, that was the rule. But Jesus had cured this man – wasn't that 'work'? – on the Sabbath day. He had broken God's law. He couldn't be a good man.

They questioned the man born blind.

'He put some mud on my eyes. I washed my face – and now I can see.'

The Pharisees didn't believe him. So they questioned his parents.

'Is this really your son? Is it true he was born blind?'

'Yes. Yes,' they said. 'But we don't know how he's been cured. He's a grown man. Ask him.' They were frightened by all the fierce questions.

'Promise to God you'll tell the truth,' the Pharisees said to the man born blind. 'The man who cured you can't be from God. He has broken God's law.'

'I don't know about that,' answered the man. 'One thing I *do* know. I was blind – and now I can see. Have you ever heard of a blind man being cured like that? If you ask me, this man must come from God. How could he do it otherwise?'

Then the Pharisees said a terrible thing.

'If you and your parents were good people, you wouldn't have been born blind. Who do you think you are, trying to teach us?' And they threw him out.

When Jesus heard what had happened he went to find the man born blind.

'Do you believe God sent me?' he asked.

'Yes, I do,' said the man – and he knelt at Jesus' feet.

'I am the light of the world,' Jesus said. 'No one who follows me will ever be left in the dark. I came to this world to open blind eyes. But some who can see have made themselves blind.' (He was talking about the Pharisees.)

'My Little Girl is Ill'

Jesus was standing on the lake-shore one day, surrounded by a crowd of people, when Jairus, one of the
leaders of the local synagogue, came hurrying towards
him. Jairus was an important man and the crowd made
way for him. As soon as he reached Jesus he threw
himself at his feet and pleaded with him, his eyes full of
tears.

'My little girl is dreadfully sick. She's only twelve and
we are so frightened for her. We love her very much.
Please come and make her well. We know you can. If
you don't come she'll die.'

'Of course I'll come,' Jesus said. 'Don't worry.' And
they began to walk towards Jairus's house. With such a
crowd it was slow going, and they were only half-way
when the messengers came running.

'Your little girl has died,' they told Jairus. 'There's
no need to bother the Teacher now.'

But Jesus didn't pay any attention to what they said.
He spoke gently to Jairus: 'Don't be afraid. Just trust
me.'

Then he sent everyone away, except three of his

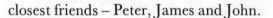

closest friends – Peter, James and John.

When they reached Jairus's house there was such a fuss. All the friends and relations were there, weeping and wailing – such a noise as you'd never believe (that's what happens in the East when someone dies).

'Why all this fuss?' Jesus said. 'Why are you crying? The little girl isn't dead – she's just asleep.'

They laughed at him.

'Do you think we don't know when someone's dead? Of course she's dead. Don't be silly!'

Jesus made them all go outside. Then he took the mother and father and his three friends to the little girl's room.

She lay there, quiet and still; not breathing. She really was dead.

Then Jesus took her by the hand.

'Little girl, get up!' he said.

She sighed. Her cheeks flushed pink, and she opened her eyes. Then she got up and walked!

Her mother and father could not believe their eyes. Jesus had brought their little girl back to life.

'Don't tell anyone about it,' he said. 'Just give her something to eat. She's hungry.'

Peter, James and John never forgot that day. Later, when Jesus said: 'I am the resurrection and the life. Whoever believes in me will live, even though he dies,' it was easy to believe his promise. Hadn't they seen living proof?

The Sheep
that Wandered Away

Jesus came to our world with a message from God for everyone. He came to show us what God is like. But that didn't mean a lot of boring lessons. When Jesus wanted people to remember what he said, he told them stories – stories with a point.

One day some of the Pharisees were grumbling about Jesus.

'He mixes with some funny people,' they said. 'A lot of no-goods.'

So Jesus told them this story.

'Pretend you're a shepherd,' he said, 'like that man on the hill over there. You have a hundred sheep. Every night you count them into the sheep-pen: "One, two, three ... ninety-seven, ninety-eight, ninety-nine, a hundred. All safe and sound." But one night when you count them in – "One, two, three ... ninety-seven, ninety-eight, ninety-nine ... Hey! There's one missing!"

'Do you go home to bed because you still have ninety-nine sheep? Isn't that enough? Of course not! You think of the one that's wandered off. Maybe it's hurt. Maybe some wild animal's attacked it.

'You make the ninety-nine sheep safe, and you go in

search of the one that has wandered away. You go on and on, calling and looking, looking and calling. And when you hear that faint answering bleat you're the happiest man on earth.

'Tired as you are, you pick up the sheep and carry it home across your shoulders. When it's safe in the sheep-pen you wake everyone up. "Let's have a celebration," you say. "I'm so happy. I've found the sheep that wandered away."

'Well,' Jesus said, 'that's what it's like in heaven when someone who has wandered away from God is brought back home.'

Jesus talked about sheep and shepherds another day.

'I am the good shepherd,' he said, 'ready to die for my sheep. I know every one of them, and they know me. They know the sound of my voice. They wouldn't follow a stranger. But they will follow me. They know I will look after them and lead them to good pasture. I am the good shepherd, ready to die for my sheep.' (He was talking about everyone who follows him.)

Will You Come
to the Wedding?

'Once upon a time,' Jesus said, 'there was a great king. He was getting everything ready for the wedding of his son the prince. You can just imagine all the preparations!' And he told this story . . .

The wedding was a grand affair, with hundreds of guests, and food to make your mouth water. The cooks had been busy for weeks. There were special cakes and pastries and an ox-roast. At last everything was ready, and the king sent his servants to tell the guests. (The invitations had been sent out months before.)

'Everything's ready. Come and enjoy the wedding feast,' he said.

But the guests were very rude. One after the other they made excuses not to go.

One said: 'I've bought a piece of land. I have to go and inspect it. Please accept my apologies.'

Another said: 'I've bought five pairs of oxen for ploughing. I must try them out. Please accept my apologies.'

A third said: 'I've just got married myself. I can't

possibly leave my wife.' (He didn't ask if she could go too! And he didn't bother to say he was sorry.)

When the king heard all these excuses he was hurt and angry.

'Well, if the official guests won't come, I'm not going to waste all this good food. Go into the town,' he said to his servants, 'and invite the poor and the blind and those who are handicapped.'

They did as he said. But there was room for more. So they went out to the country roads and lanes and invited everyone they met – till the king's palace was full.

The king welcomed them all. 'I tell you,' he said, 'not one of my official guests shall taste this dinner.' And he closed the doors.

'God is sending you an invitation,' Jesus said to the people who were listening to the story. 'He is inviting you to his kingdom, as his guests. Make sure you say yes. If you don't he will ask others in your place.'

The Farmer
and the Seeds

'There was once a farmer,' Jesus said, 'who went to his field to sow seed. He walked to and fro on the soft brown soil and scattered handfuls of seeds evenly across the ground.

'But some seeds fell on the path. And as soon as the farmer had gone the birds swooped down and gobbled them up.

'Some seeds fell on rocky ground where the soil was thin. The seeds soon sprouted, but the roots couldn't go deep. So the hot sun made the young plants wilt and die.

'Some seeds fell among the thorns and they choked the young plants.

'But the seeds that fell on the ploughed land, where the soil was deep, took root and grew – green at first, then gold, with heavy heads of grain. At harvest time some of those seeds produced a hundred new grains, some sixty, some thirty.

'If you have ears to hear with, listen and understand,' Jesus said to the crowd. (It was another of his stories with a point.)

Later, Jesus' friends asked him to explain.

'I wasn't really talking about farming,' Jesus said. 'The farmer and his seed is a picture of what happens when people listen to God's message – the message I have come to bring.

'Some listen, but don't understand at all. It makes no difference to them. It's as if the birds came and gobbled up the seed.

'Others listen eagerly and seem to take it in. But their interest doesn't last. When problems come, they just give up. The seed has fallen on shallow, rocky soil.

'Then there are those who are so taken up with the worries and cares of life, and with getting rich, that the message is choked – like the seeds that fell among the thorns.

'But some people are ready and eager for God's message. They hear and understand and take it in – and their lives are changed. They are like the grain that comes to harvest.'

Jesus came with an invitation to God's kingdom. He used a lot of pictures to describe it.

'It's like a pearl,' he said, 'the biggest, most beautiful pearl you can think of. If you traded in pearls you would sell everything you have to buy it.'

'It's like buried treasure. If you were digging in someone's field one day and found treasure, you'd sell everything you have to buy the field and make the treasure yours.'

'It's more important than anything else to belong to God's kingdom, to be one of his people. And everyone's invited.'

The Big Spender

Jesus was always getting into trouble for making the wrong friends. At least, that's what the Pharisees thought. If they had had their way he would only have spoken to good people. But Jesus wanted to help everyone who needed him. So he told the Pharisees this story.

There was once a man who had two sons. The younger one was bored, living at home and working all day on the farm. He wanted to see the world. So he said to his father:

'Dad, I know half the farm will be mine when you die. But I'll be old by then. I'd like to have my share now.'

His father felt hurt. But he divided the farm in two and the younger boy sold his half and went abroad. He really lived it up. He had a good time. But when all the money was spent, his new friends soon went away.

There was no food to buy and the boy had nothing. He got a job looking after some pigs. He was so hungry he would have been glad to eat the bean-pods they fed to the pigs!

He had plenty of time to think. And one day he said to

himself: 'This is very silly. Here I am, starving – and at home even the servants have more than they can eat. I'll tell Dad I'm sorry. I'll ask him to take me on as one of his workers.'

That same day he started for home. He was still quite a long way away when his father saw him coming. He'd watched the road every day, just in case. He ran to meet his son and hugged him so tight that he could hardly breathe!

'I'm sorry, Dad,' the boy said, as soon as he could speak. 'I've been very wrong. I'm not fit to be your son.'

But his father was so glad to see him, he shouted to his servants: 'Bring the best suit of clothes and a ring for his finger – and shoes. And we'll kill the prize calf. Let's have a celebration. My boy was as good as dead, but he's alive. He was lost, but now he's found.'

*

When the older son came home from a hard day's work in the fields he couldn't imagine what had happened. The whole house was in an uproar. And there was a marvellous smell of roasting meat.

'What's going on?' he asked one of the servants.

'Haven't you heard? Your brother's come home. And there's to be a party. Your father's killed the prize calf.'

When the older brother heard that, he was so angry he stormed out of the house. That selfish young brat. What had *he* ever done to deserve this?

His father tried to calm him down.

'My brother sold half the farm and spent all your money. And you want me to celebrate! When did you ever give *me* a party?'

'But everything I have is yours,' his father said. 'We have to be happy today. Your brother was as good as dead, but he's alive. He was lost, but now he's found.'

The Man
the Robbers Set On

A man pushed his way through the crowd. He wanted to ask Jesus a question.

'Teacher,' he said, 'the Bible says that if I want to please God I must love him with all my heart and mind; and I must love other people as I love myself.'

'That's right,' Jesus said.

'But what does it mean?'

The man who was asking the question was a teacher himself. He was trying to trick Jesus. So Jesus did not answer; instead he told this story.

'There was a man who went on a journey from Jerusalem to Jericho. He passed the last house and soon the road was winding steeply down through bare hills. It was lonely, with no one else in sight.

'All of a sudden the man was jumped on by a gang of robbers. They took everything he had and beat him up. Then they made off. He was left lying by the road, too badly hurt to move. The fierce sun beat down and the man groaned.

'Not long after, someone came by. He was a priest.

When he saw the man lying there it really upset him.

'That might have been me, he thought. Good thing I didn't start out sooner. He glanced nervously round, then hurried past, on the other side of the road.

'The next person to come along was a Levite who worked in God's temple. He went across to look at the wounded man. But he didn't stop either. He hurried past, on the other side of the road.

'The third man who came by was a Samaritan.'

Jesus paused. He knew how everyone felt about the Samaritans. Though they were neighbours, living in the same country, no Jew would so much as speak to one of them. Samaritans were foreigners; they didn't believe the right things.

Jesus went on: 'The Samaritan saw the man lying there. What a rotten thing to happen, he said to himself. That might have been me. I must see what I can do to help.

'He unstrapped the saddlebag from his donkey and took out a flask of olive oil and some wine. He used them to clean the man's cuts. Gently he bandaged the wounds. Then he put the man on his donkey and took him to the nearest inn. He put him to bed and made him comfortable for the night.

'Next day he had to leave. But before he went he gave the innkeeper some money.

'"Take good care of him," he said. "And if that's not enough I'll pay you the rest when I come back."

'Now then,' said Jesus to the teacher. 'What do you think? Which of those three men do you think really loved the man the robbers beat up?'

'The one who was kind to him,' the teacher answered. (He couldn't bear to say 'the Samaritan'.)

'You are right,' Jesus said. 'God wants us to be like that man. We're not allowed to pick and choose; we are to love everyone. That means we must be kind to *anyone* who needs our help.'

The Little Man
who Climbed a Tree

One day Jesus went to Jericho. There was a man called Zacchaeus living there. He was very rich – but he wasn't honest. He collected taxes for the Romans and made a lot of money for himself. Zacchaeus wasn't much to look at. He was very short – and rather stout.

Zacchaeus had heard that Jesus was coming. The whole town was buzzing with the news. Everyone said what a wonderful man he was. Most people knew someone he had made well. And what a teacher! There was no one like him. So Zacchaeus had made up his mind to see Jesus. But what chance was there, with all those crowds?

Zacchaeus was far too short to see over people's heads. And no one would let him through – they all hated him. Everyone knew how he made his money – playing up to the Romans and cheating his own people. If only he could think of a way.

Then he had a brainwave. He ran ahead of the crowd and climbed a tree that overhung the road. Jesus walked right under that tree and Zacchaeus had a grandstand view.

Then something happened that Zacchaeus had not bargained for. He almost fell off the branch in surprise. Jesus stopped right under his tree and looked up.

'Come on down, Zacchaeus. And be quick about it. I'm coming to stay at your house today.'

Zacchaeus couldn't believe his ears. Jesus knew his name. Jesus, of all people, was treating him like a

friend. He couldn't get over it. Most people crossed the road when they saw Zacchaeus coming!

Zacchaeus gave Jesus such a welcome! A lot of people grumbled about it, of course. How could Jesus – a good man if ever there was one – have anything to do with that cheat?

But Zacchaeus was never the same again. That meeting with Jesus was the most important moment in his life. After dinner – and a very good dinner it was – Zacchaeus stood up in front of all his guests and made a speech.

'Sir,' he said, turning to Jesus, 'I'm not a good man. I've robbed and cheated. I've taken money from people who couldn't afford it. But since you came to my house all that's changed. I'll never cheat anyone again. I want to put things right, so I'll give half my money to help the poor, and those I've cheated I will repay four times over.'

There was a stunned silence as he sat down.

Then Jesus spoke.

'A life has been saved in this house today. Zacchaeus has decided to live as God wants. This is what I came for – to look for those who have lost their way, and bring them back to God.'

Long Live the King!

It was spring. Groups of pilgrims were making their way to Jerusalem for the Passover Festival. Jesus thought back to the time he was twelve. How excited he'd been when Mary and Joseph brought him to Jerusalem for the very first time. Now he felt sad. He knew this visit would be his last. For three years he had travelled and taught. He had made many friends – but he had enemies too. It was dangerous to come to Jerusalem. But if that was what God wanted . . .

'I am the good shepherd,' he murmured softly to himself, 'ready to die for the sheep.'

His friends looked at him anxiously. They knew his life was in danger. For three years they had been with him, listening to him, watching all he did. Now there was no doubt in their minds. Jesus was no ordinary man. He was God's Son, the promised King, come to set God's people free.

But when? That was the question Judas kept asking. When would Jesus start the revolution and throw out the Romans? He didn't understand.

*

They were nearly there.

'Go to the next village,' Jesus said to two of his friends. 'You'll find a donkey tied up, with her colt. Bring them to me. If anyone asks what you are doing, say "the Teacher needs them".'

They did as he said. The colt had never been ridden before. But it stood quite still as Jesus got on. He stroked the rough mane and spoke in soothing tones.

As they rounded the hill the great temple came in sight, and Jesus broke down and cried. Jerusalem, the city of God – he loved it so much. But the people would not listen to God's message. And so Jerusalem would be destroyed. Roman soldiers would break down the walls. The temple would be torn down stone by stone.

But what was that noise? Jesus' friends shaded their eyes as they looked down the road. A great crowd of

people was coming out to meet them, shouting and waving branches of palm.

Excitedly they lined the route as the King rode in – a king of peace, riding a donkey not a war-horse. Cloaks and branches of palm were spread in his path. The procession grew and grew: men, women and children, all shouting and singing.

'Long live the King! God bless the King of Israel, the one whom God has promised!'

The whole city was in an uproar.

'Who is it?' strangers asked.

'It's Jesus, from Nazareth in Galilee,' came the reply.

As soon as he could Jesus went to the temple. Inside the great courtyards were stalls where men were selling pigeons to those who could not afford a more expensive offering to give to God. The money-changers at their tables counted out the special temple coins in exchange for the everyday ones. They were cheating their customers. The noise was deafening.

When Jesus saw all this he was very angry. He strode to the nearest table and turned it upside-down. The money-changer scrambled for his spilled coins.

'God says his temple is a house of prayer,' Jesus stormed above the hubbub. 'But you have turned it into a robbers' den.'

Judas

Judas was angry and upset. Why hadn't Jesus started the revolution the day he rode into the city? He had missed his best chance. Wasn't he going to free his people from the Romans? Wasn't he going to be that kind of king?

Judas felt let down. That was why he went to see the priests – the ones who wanted Jesus killed. That was why Judas agreed to betray his friend, to hand Jesus over in some quiet place where there were no crowds to defend him. That was why Judas took the thirty silver coins the priests agreed to pay him.

Jesus and his friends spent each night in the village of Bethany, at the house of Mary and Martha and their brother Lazarus. Each day Jesus went into the city and talked to the crowds and healed the sick, as he always did. Before the week was over Judas would betray him. Jesus knew that. He didn't need anyone to tell him. He had always been able to read people's thoughts.

On the last night of his life Jesus and his friends found a room in Jerusalem where they could share the special Passover meal. Everything was ready.

They sat down to eat. Before the meal was over Judas slipped out into the night. Only Jesus knew that he had gone to fetch the guards.

Then, Jesus took a loaf of bread, gave thanks, and broke it in his hands, sharing it around.

'My body,' he said, 'that is broken for you.'

Then he took a cup of wine, gave thanks again, and passed it around.

'My blood,' he said, 'that is spilled for you and for many, to bring you God's forgiveness.'

No one quite understood, but they all felt sad. Jesus talked until it was late, trying to prepare his friends for the terrible days ahead.

'Although I'm going away, I'll come back,' he said. 'That's a promise. And when I'm gone I shall send God's Holy Spirit to strengthen and help you.'

'I won't let you go,' Peter said. 'I'll never leave you.'

Sadly Jesus said to him, 'Peter, before the cock crows at dawn you will say three times you do not know me.'

It was time to go. They walked through the dark night to a place they loved on the way to Bethany – the olive-orchard of Gethsemane. (Judas had counted on them stopping there.) Jesus took Peter, James and John in with him, under the trees. The others stayed near the gate.

'Keep watch with me,' Jesus said. Then he began to pray, in great distress. He knew he was going to die.

'Father, if it's possible, spare my life. But only if that's what you want . . .'

Three times he prayed. Three times, when he went back to his friends, he found them asleep.

Then there were voices and the flickering light of torches. Judas had come with a band of armed men to arrest him.

'The one I kiss on the cheek is the one you want,' he said. And he went up to Jesus and kissed him.

Sentence of Death

The armed guard hurried Jesus through the sleeping streets. At the house of the High Priest lamps were burning and the Council had been summoned. Peter followed at a safe distance – all the others had run away. They took Jesus inside and Peter hung about in the courtyard. It was cold and he edged nearer to the fire. A servant-girl passed.

'Aren't you a friend of the man they've arrested?' she said.

Peter had never felt so frightened. He shrank back into the shadows. 'No! No! You've made a mistake. I don't know the man.'

Three times that night the same question was asked. Each time Peter made the same reply.

'I don't know the man. I don't know the man.'

Then, as dawn broke, he heard a cock crow – and Peter remembered Jesus' words. He went away, sobbing as if his heart would break.

Inside the house the Council were having a hard time of it. The prisoner would not answer their questions. He just stood there, not saying a word. Even when they hit him he made no move to defend himself.

The witnesses they had dragged from their beds could not agree. The Council could not make their charges stick.

Almost in despair the High Priest turned to Jesus.

'In God's name, tell us: are you the promised King, the Son of God?'

'I am,' Jesus said. 'One day everyone will know, when you see me seated at God's right hand and coming with the clouds of heaven.'

'Enough!' shouted the High Priest. 'He is speaking against God. That is blasphemy.'

'We find the prisoner guilty,' said the Council. And they sentenced him to death.

But there was still one problem. They had to get the Roman Governor's consent. They took Jesus to Pilate.

'This man is guilty of treason,' they said. 'He has tried to make himself king.' They knew the Roman Emperor wouldn't like that! Pilate would have to take the matter seriously.

'Are you the king of the Jews?' Pilate asked Jesus. But there was no reply.

Every Passover Pilate set one of his prisoners free. So he went outside and spoke to the crowd.

'Shall I set free your king?'

'No!' they shouted back. 'We want Barabbas.' (He was a murderer.)

'Then what shall I do with Jesus?'

'Crucify him! Crucify him!'

Pilate washed his hands of the affair. If that was what they wanted . . . He handed Jesus over to his soldiers and they took him away. Then they began to make fun of him. They dressed him up in a purple robe and gave him a crown of sharp thorns. Then he was whipped and made to carry the wooden beam of the cross to Skull Hill. There they crucified him, with two thieves, one on either side.

'Father, forgive them,' Jesus prayed, as he hung there in great pain. Then, with a loud cry – 'It is finished!' – he died.

Two secret friends of Jesus begged Pilate for the body. Hurriedly they buried him in a new tomb, cut out of the rock. They rolled a great stone across the entrance to seal it.

The Body
that Wasn't There!

Jesus died on Friday afternoon. For three hours the sun was blotted out and the whole land was dark. The Roman soldiers, used to seeing prisoners die, had seen nothing like this before. 'It must have been true,' said the officer in charge. 'This man really was the Son of God.'

Saturday was the Sabbath, the day of the Festival and a day of rest. All was quiet.

But on Sunday morning the women got up early – as soon as it was light. Three of them hurried to the tomb, carrying sweet-smelling spices. (There had been so little time on Friday, when Jesus' body was buried.) The spices were to put on the body – if only they could roll away the stone.

To their surprise, when they got there, the stone was already rolled back – and there was someone sitting there, dressed all in white.

'Don't be afraid,' he said. 'I know you are looking for Jesus. But he's not here. He's alive! Go and tell all his friends – especially Peter.'

Mary Magdalene took in only one thing. The body

had gone. She ran to find Peter, arriving all out of breath.

'Peter! John! They've taken Jesus away!'

The two friends set off at a run. John got there first. He stopped and looked in. There were the strips of cloth they had wound round the body, and the cloth for his head. He waited for Peter to catch up. Then they both went inside. The wrappings were all in place – they hadn't been taken off the body. There was just no body inside them.

Then they knew! The body wasn't there – because Jesus was alive again. He'd come back as he had promised.

A little later, Mary returned; she had followed slowly. She stood outside the tomb, crying. Through her tears she saw two angels dressed in white where the body of Jesus had been.

'Why are you crying?' they asked.

'Because they've taken Jesus away.'

She turned and caught a glimpse of someone. Perhaps it was the gardener. He would know.

'If you took him away, please tell me where he is.'

'Mary!'

As soon as she heard his voice, she *knew*!

'Teacher!' she said – her heart so full of joy she thought it would burst.

Late that evening Jesus' friends were together behind locked doors. Suddenly Jesus was there in the room with them. He showed them the marks on his hands and feet, where the nails had fastened him to the cross. Then they knew it was him. He was real! He was alive! They were too glad even to speak!

Thomas wasn't there that night.

'I don't believe it,' he said when they told him what had happened. 'Dead men don't come back to life. I *won't* believe unless I see the marks of the nails and touch the scars myself.'

A week later, Jesus came again. He held out his hands for Thomas to see. But there was no need. Thomas was kneeling at Jesus' feet.

'My Lord and my God!' he said.

Good News for Everyone

The friends of Jesus saw him several times after that first wonderful reunion on Easter Sunday. Once they were fishing on Lake Galilee. They had been out all night and at dawn they saw someone standing on the beach.

'Have you caught any fish?'

'Not one!' they called back.

'Throw your nets to the right.'

Suddenly the nets were full of fish!

John said, 'It's Jesus!' And Peter's mind flew back to the time he had first met Jesus: what a catch he had made that day.

He jumped straight overboard and swam ashore, leaving the others to bring in the catch.

There was a small fire burning, cooking some fish – and bread all ready for a picnic breakfast – the best they had ever tasted. Their happiest times were spent with Jesus.

After breakfast Jesus asked Peter if he really loved him. He asked him *three times*! Peter felt hurt. Surely Jesus didn't need to ask; it made him think of the dreadful night when he had said three times that he didn't know Jesus.

'You *know* I love you,' Peter said.

'Then there's a special job for you to do. Take care of my sheep when I'm gone.' Peter knew that Jesus meant the little group of his followers – and he was happy again.

Not long after this Jesus left them to return to his Father in heaven. They did not see him again, though they knew they would one day. He had promised to come back.

Meantime there was work to do. They must tell everyone about him. They must spread the good news that Jesus had come to bring forgiveness and new life to everyone who believed in him. That was why he had to die. He took our punishment. Now no one needs to be afraid of death. Jesus is alive!

All through Jerusalem and the land of Israel – out to the farthest corners of the Roman Empire – the good news spread.

Good news for everyone, everywhere.
Good news then.
Good news now!

Jesus said:

'Let the children come to me
    and do not stop them,
because the Kingdom of heaven
    belongs to such as these.'